FOUR AMERICAN INDIAN
LITERARY MASTERS

FOUR AMERICAN INDIAN LITERARY MASTERS

N. Scott Momaday
James Welch
Leslie Marmon Silko, and
Gerald Vizenor

By Alan R. Velie

UNIVERSITY OF OKLAHOMA PRESS : NORMAN

By Alan R. Velie

Shakespeare's Repentance Plays: The Search for an Adequate Form (Cranbury, N.J., 1972)

Blood and Knavery: A Collection of English Renaissance Pamphlets and Ballads of Crime and Sin (with Joseph H. Marshburn; Cranbury, N.J., 1973)

Appleseeds and Beercans: Man and Nature in Literature (Pacific Palisades, Calif., 1974)

American Indian Literature: An Anthology (Norman, 1979)

Four American Indian Literary Masters: N. Scott Momaday, James Welch, Leslie Marmon Silko, and Gerald Vizenor (Norman, 1982)

Library of Congress Cataloging in Publication Data

Velie, Alan R., 1937-
    Four American Indian literary masters.
    Bibliography: p. 159
    Includes index.
    1. American literature—Indian authors—History and criticism. I. Title.
PS508.I5V4   810'.9'897   81-43642
                   AACR2

To Sue, Jon, and Will

CONTENTS

PREFACE

I BEGAN TEACHING Indian literature in the fall of 1971 in response to a request by a delegation of Indian students. During that period of student unrest there were frequent demands for "relevant" courses. I had been serving on a committee studying the possibility of a black studies program at Oklahoma. Perhaps that is where the students got my name; they did not say, and I had never seen any of them before. Oklahoma Indians were not generally militant, and this group did not make the threats and nonnegotiable demands so common at the time; they merely asked whether I would be interested in teaching a course about Indian literature. I was interested, but my specialty was Shakespeare, and I knew very little about Indian literature. They said that no one else seemed to know anything at all and that they hoped I could organize such a course before the term got under way. I agreed, with the understanding that I would first teach it only to Indian students, who realized that I was a novice, and not display my limitations any more widely than necessary in an experimental course hurriedly put together. The course went as well as I could expect, and I have been teaching it ever since to all comers.

From the beginning the course evoked enough interest that the public relations department at my university issued a press release describing its subject and goals. Although I doubt it was the first course of its kind in the country, it was novel enough for the story to be picked up by the Associated Press, and it ran in scores of newspapers around the country, including *The New York Times*. That may have spurred some additional interest in the course; I got a number of letters from teachers asking for bibliographies and advice. In any case, the time had come for Indian literature, and soon there were scores of such courses around the country, particularly in the West, where most of America's Indians live.

Although there is no shortage of traditional and transitional literature, most of the material in the course I teach is contemporary American Indian literature — poetry, fiction, and drama written by college-educated Indians who speak no language but English and who are part of the American literary community. My reason for emphasizing contemporary Indian writers is that my training and knowledge of the earlier literature is only marginal. Anthropologists, it seems to me, are the best teachers of myths. I have wrestled with Claude Levi-Strauss's *Mythologiques* in an attempt to break the code of some of the arcane tales, and I am familiar with Alan Dundes's work on structural typology.[1] Although I manage to carry on at some length in class and put a good many terms on the board during our discussions, I usually have the feeling that I am poaching on someone else's preserve when I teach myths. I feel (even more keenly) that the songs, or chants, require the expertise of a musicologist. In my anthology, *American Indian Literature*,[2] I included the music with the text, though I do not even read music myself. I play tapes to the students and talk about the words as poetry, but I have no illusions that I am doing justice to the material. Having been through Quintilian and Cicero under different auspices, I have something to say about oratory, but not as much as I might. I can treat the memoirs as species of biography well enough, but a historian would be better able to discuss the events these narratives describe.

So it is with great relief that I reach modern literature, and I reach it as soon as I can. Accordingly, it is modern Indian literature that is the focus of this book—the work of four well-known Indian writers—Scott Momaday, James Welch, Leslie Silko, and Gerald Vizenor.

FOUR AMERICAN INDIAN
LITERARY MASTERS

Chapter 1

INTRODUCTION

THE PURPOSE of this book is to introduce readers to four outstanding American Indian writers—N. Scott Momaday, James Welch, Leslie Marmon Silko, and Gerald Vizenor. It is designed both for teachers of Indian literature and for readers generally who would like to know more about the literature of one of our least understood ethnic groups. Before I turn to these authors, however, I would like to make a few statements about the traditional forms of Indian literature and indicate what I think are the most limiting misconceptions of it among non-Indian readers.

Courses in Indian literature are a recent addition to college curricula. To judge from the anthologies that serve as texts, their content is usually pretty standard. The course proceeds chronologically, beginning with myths and legends—those traditional narratives of the tribes that have been translated from the original language. These were originally as much a species of drama as of fiction, and much of their interest is lost when they are transliterated into an English prose form. Some teachers recognize this; some do not. Most of us, however, feel that it is better to teach them, even if they are maimed, than to ignore them. Next come the songs, which are printed in college texts as poetry because, without their music, they look something like Haiku verses. To see translations of these songs as two- or three-line poems, when their performance, to the accompaniment of drums, flutes, and rattles, requires several hours, is something like reducing an opera to the program notes. Once again, however, they should not be ignored.

Following the songs in the standard anthologies is a section on what might be termed transitional literature—works by Indians, often written in an Indian language, that are intended to be read by whites. Oratory and memoirs are the two main genres here. The same speeches seem to appear in every collection: Red Jacket's answer to Missionary Cram and Seattle's surrender, along with speeches by Sitting Bull, Pontiac, and Tecumseh. Apparently the most popular memoirs are those of the Sioux medicine men Black Elk and Lame Deer and of the Apache chiefs Geronimo and Cochise.

Contemporary Indian writers are generally represented in literature courses by poetry and fiction, the staple genres of English department curricula. Nevertheless, there are problems of modern terminology and some popular misconceptions that must be dealt with.

My first concern is with the word *Indian*. I have seen books and articles that use the terms *Amerindian* and *Native American*. I am not sure where these terms came from; I would guess that white academics, or possibly Indian academics, made them up. I have never heard an Indian outside the university community call himself anything but an Indian. This may not be so in parts of the country where there are reservations (Oklahoma has none; most Indians live in towns) or in cities where Indians are not living with their tribes, but to my knowledge Indians only use the term *Indian*. I lived for years in Little Axe, Oklahoma, a small community some twenty miles east of Norman, in which the population is approximately 40 percent Shawnee and the rest primarily white, with a small number of blacks and Indians of other tribes. The Indians I talked to, including the tribal leaders, had never heard of an Amerindian or Native American; certainly they never used these terms.

Another popular misconception—not quite so widely held now as it was a few years ago, but still prevalent among both whites and Indians—is that Indian literature, if it exists at all, is at best rudimentary, consisting mainly of stories for children. Many people are aware that Indian

5

culture was preliterate, and they erroneously assume that it could not have produced much of what we call literature. Accustomed to thinking of Indians as people in a plight, they imagined that a full schedule of suffering had not permitted Indians to write much. Indian culture had a very rich oral tradition, and anyone familiar with the *Odyssey* and the *Iliad* knows that poetry and narration transmitted orally are by no means inferior to written language. Plight or no plight, Momaday's *House Made of Dawn* won the Pulitzer Prize, and Welch's *Winter in the Blood* was reviewed on the first page of the *New York Times Book Review*.

A more bothersome misconception, or habit of mind, is the tendency of white Americans to read any book by an Indian about Indians as protest literature—that is, as essentially a political work championing Indians against their brutal enemies, white Americans. It is condescending to make this assumption; it implies that Indians are not to determine their own attitudes about life in America and are required to concentrate their efforts on reviling the whites.

Readers seldom expect novels by Jewish authors like Philip Roth, Saul Bellow, and Bernard Malamud to be protest novels; they accept them pretty much on the authors' own terms. Most readers recognize comic novels by Jewish authors as comic and are not surprised to see Jews taking a comic view toward contemporary life. The same readers seem reluctant to grant Indians or blacks the same freedom. Black poet Al Young ridicules this attitude:

> Dont nobody want no nice nigger no more
> these honkies man that put out
> these books and things
> they want an angry splib
> a furious nigrah
> they dont want no bourgeois woogie
> they want them a militant nigger
> in a fiji haircut

fresh out of some secret boot camp
with a bad book in one hand
and a molotov cocktail in the other
subject to turn up at one of their conferences
or soirees
and shake the shit out of them[1]

Blackfeet poet and novelist James Welch concurs with the idea that by and large whites expect minority writers to be militant protesters:

I have seen poems about Indians written by whites and they are either sentimental or outraged over the condition of the Indian. . . . for the most part only an Indian knows who he is—an individual who just happens to be Indian. . . . And hopefully he will have the toughness and fairness to present his material in a way that is not manufactured by a conventional stance.[2]

It is curious, but, given the nature of the American publishing industry, militance is commercial, and anger, not complacency, is the "conventional stance" expected of blacks and Indians by the literary world. Welch, Momaday, Silko, and Vizenor have avoided this conventional stance, even though they are often angered by bigotry. Although their books are complex and honest, readers often reduce them to simpleminded melodramas that pit red against white, with the red men wearing the white hats—the simple obverse of the horse opera of decent settler pitted against bloodthirsty Comanche.

Later I will discuss these questions at length, but let me here provide an example of what I mean. The protagonist of *House Made of Dawn* is identified only as Abel; we never learn his last name. One does not have to be a deep reader to recognize this obvious bit of symbolism, although I must point out that it takes a bit of prodding to get most students, even in the Bible Belt, to remember Abel as the archetypal victim. Once that is established, the question is, Who is the Cain who strikes Abel down? The answer the students invariably give is white society. In fact, though, none of the three men who do this Abel the most harm is white. Juan Fragua, the albino, is a Tanoan; Tosamah is a Kiowa with a suspicious resemblance to Momaday himself; and Martinez is either a Chicano or an Indian with a Spanish surname. Long before Abel was buffeted by the white world, he was rejected by his own tribe because he was illegitimate. Thus the source of Abel's troubles is complex. Whites are by no means blameless, but it is a superficial reader who calls the book a protest novel. I make the same point in chapters 4 and 6 about *Winter in the Blood* and *Ceremony*. This sort of misreading not only distorts the authors' racial attitudes but also undervalues their works as literature. *Uncle Tom's Cabin* may have helped the cause of abolition immensely, but it is not great literature. James Baldwin makes this point forcefully in his essay "Everybody's Protest Novel": *"Uncle Tom's Cabin* is a very bad novel, having, in its self-righteous, virtuous sentimentality, much in common with *Little Women."*[3] Lest it seem that Baldwin is objecting only to protest novels by whites about blacks, it is important to note that he had the same objections to Richard Wright's *Native Son:*

> Bigger [the hero of *Native Son*] is Uncle Tom's descendant, flesh of his flesh, so exactly opposite a portrait that the contemporary Negro novelist and the dead New England woman are locked together in a deadly, timeless battle; the one uttering merciless exhortations, the other shouting curses.[4]

According to Baldwin, the problem with these and all other protest novels is that in the name of bringing freedom to the oppressed they perpetuate racial stereotypes. "Our passion for categorization," he says, "life neatly fitted into pegs [*sic*] has led to unforeseen, paradoxical distress; confusion, a breakdown of meaning."[5] The essence of Baldwin's objections to protest novels is that, first, they diminish the humanity of both the minority and the majority, and, second, they confuse literature with sociology; writers with good intentions are not the same as good writers.

Unfortunately, blacks and Indians are stereotyped by the left as well as by the right. Ishmael Reed tells of being denied the opportunity to teach black literature at West Coast College when he refused to make it an exercise in radical politics.[6] In Reed's eyes these radicals were just as rigid in their racism as are reactionaries.

Another point worth mentioning concerns tribal identities. Most Indians identify themselves as members of particular tribes. It is true that some urban Indians have lost their tribal identity, and Indian college students largely ignore tribe and use the term *Skins* to speak of other Indians, but for most Indians today the groups from which they derive their ethnic identity are their tribal groups—the Shawnees, Cherokees, or Apaches—not "Indians" as a whole. In Oklahoma, for instance, working-class Indians (and this means the vast majority) often will not take a better job in another part of the state if they believe that the Indians there will not accept them.

It makes more sense to compare Indians with Europeans. Europeans think of themselves not as an undifferentiated lot but, rather, as Portuguese, Swedes, Hungarians, Italians, and so on. Although most Europeans are ultimately descended from the same stock—the Aryan, or Indo-European, linguistic group—there are differences in culture, language, and, to some extent, stature and pigmentation. So it is with Indians. When Columbus came to America, there were more than two thousand independent tribes, of which more than three hundred have survived. These tribes spoke five hundred languages belonging to fifty language groups, some of them as unlike as English and Polish. The Algonquian peoples of the Northeast, the Civilized Tribes of the Southeast, the Sioux Nations of the plains, and the

Pueblos of the Southwest had different histories, cultures, and religions.

The major focus of this book will be to show how contemporary Indian writers have drawn on their tribal heritage and how they have been affected by modern American and European literary movements. I will examine Momaday's Kiowa heritage, his boyhood experiences among the Tanoans, and the influence of Yvor Winters and the post-symbolists in his poetry. With Welch I will look at Blackfeet mythology and South American surrealism. I will examine Silko's Laguna background and her use of myths that closely resemble the myth of the Wasteland, which is so important to twentieth-century poetry and fiction. With Vizenor I will examine the Chippewa trickster myths and "post-modern" fiction.

Chapter 2

THE SEARCH FOR IDENTITY

N. Scott Momaday's Autobiographical Works

N. Scott Momaday

ALL WRITERS draw from their lives and their experiences in creating their fictions, some to a much greater degree than others. Thomas Wolfe is probably the most autobiographical of novelists; in *Look Homeward Angel* and *You Can't Go Home Again* he did little more than change the names of people he knew to create his characters. John Hawkes, on the other hand, has the sort of mind that invents characters, events, and settings. The landscapes, people, and events in *The Lime Twig, Second Skin,* and *Death, Sleep, and the Traveller* are drawn from Hawkes's imagination rather than from his experiences.

Scott Momaday is a good deal closer to Wolfe than to Hawkes; he incorporated much of his early life in New Mexico into *House Made of Dawn.* Momaday is not at all reticent about describing his life; he has written two memoirs, *The Way to Rainy Mountain* and *The Names,* which tell us about his childhood, his intellectual development, and the heritage of his family. These works are not just important to an understanding of *House Made of Dawn;* they are exquisitely written books and well worth reading in their own right. Although *The Names* was written after *The Way to Rainy Mountain,* I will discuss it first, because in it Momaday deals more fully with his early life.

The Names is a beautiful book about a very happy childhood. Because Momaday traces his family history through four generations, *The Names* bears an obvious similarity to Alex Haley's *Roots,* though there is an important difference between the two works in tone and impact. Like Momaday, Haley had a pleasant childhood, and after the Civil War, when the survivors reached Tennessee, his family was

13

very successful indeed: Haley's grandfather owned a lumber mill and became a wealthy and influential man, respected in the white community as well as in the black. But by far the longest section of the book depicts the experiences of the family during slavery, and these experiences were very grim. Perhaps the most vivid scenes in *Roots* are those that take place aboard the slave ship. Accordingly, the book and the television programs that grew out of it showed Americans the terrible agony the blacks suffered in America.

The Names shows something very different. Although Momaday could have written about the atrocities perpetrated on the Kiowas by the cavalry, or the indignities they suffered later in western Oklahoma, he chose to put his emphasis elsewhere, and as a result the effect of *The Names* is very different but just as instructive. Most Americans are aware of the miserable treatment Indians received at the hands of the whites during the nineteenth and twentieth centuries, and when whites think of Indians they often think of Indian suffering, both past and present. Liberals tend to pity Indians for their "plight," radicals tend to emphasize the distress of the Indians to justify the need for revolution, and reactionaries look harshly down on Indian poverty and backwardness. None of these attitudes is an appropriate response to *The Names;* in fact, the general reaction to Momaday's narrative is to envy him for what he describes as the "pastoral time of my growing up."[1]

The account of his life at Jemez, New Mexico, is an idyll of feasts, ceremonies, and trips on horseback through what Momaday believes to be the most beautiful country on earth. It would be dishonest and inaccurate to deny that Indians have suffered at the hands of whites in this country, but one would be equally mistaken to believe that all Indians suffer. Momaday's book is eloquent testimony that there are Indians who live rich and happy lives both on

14

reservations and in towns with populations that are primarily white.

On his maternal side Momaday traces his family back
through four generations to his mother's great-grandparents,
I. J. Galyen, a white Kentucky settler, and Natachee, a
Cherokee whose family, unlike most other members of the
tribe, had avoided the forced march over the Trail of Tears
to Oklahoma. Momaday's mother, Natachee Scott, was
named for her great-grandmother, and although there were
no more Indians in the family in the intervening generations, Natachee began early to conceive of herself as an
Indian. As a teenager she called herself "Little Moon."

It is a curious quirk of bigotry, but in this country a
person who is an eighth black is considered simply black,
as black as someone with no white blood, but a person
who is an eighth anything else—Italian, Indian, Irish—is
hardly considered a member of that group at all. So although it may seem somewhat presumptuous that young
Natachee considered herself Indian on such slender genetic
evidence, Momaday makes the point that names play an
important role in determining who we are, and that such
an identity is largely a matter of imagination:

> That dim native heritage became a fascination and a cause
> for her, inasmuch, perhaps, as it enabled her to assume an
> attitude of defiance, an attitude which she assumed with
> particular style and satisfaction; it became her. She imag-
> ined who she was. This act of imagination was, I believe,
> among the most important events of my mother's early life,
> as later the same essential act was to be among the most
> important of my own. [P. 25]

Momaday's views on identity are strongly existential.
People create their own identity; Indians are people who
think of themselves as Indians.

Natachee took to wrapping herself in a blanket and

15

wearing a feather, and she enrolled in Haskell Institute, the Indian school at Lawrence, Kansas. There she met the girl who introduced her to her future husband, Alfred Momaday, or Huan-toa, as he was known in Kiowa.

On his father's side Momaday's forebears were Kiowas who lived the tribal life and spoke the tribal tongue. Their identity was not so much a matter of existential choice as one of genetic destiny. Momaday traces his heritage back to Kau-au-ointy, his great-great-grandmother, a remarkable woman who had been a captive and a slave. She was captured as a child in Mexico in the days when the Kiowas, whom Momaday calls "a proud race of warriors and thieves," stole not only horses but people. Kau-au-ointy outlived her slave status and married a Kiowa. Momaday describes her in *The Way to Rainy Mountain:* "She raised a lot of eyebrows they say, for she would not play the part of a Kiowa woman. From slavery she rose up to become a figure in the tribe. She owned a great herd of cattle, and she could ride as well as any man. She had blue eyes."[2]

Kau-au-ointy's grandson Mammedaty, Momaday's grandfather, was a peyote priest and a farmer. Successful farmers were rare among the Kiowas, because Kiowas had no agrarian tradition and disdained agriculture and those who practiced it—not only the whites but also Indians, such as the Wichitas and the Osages. Mammedaty was a survivor, however, and "while many of his kinsmen gave themselves up to self-pity and despair, Mammedaty sowed cotton and wheat, melon and beans" (p. 29).

But Mammedaty was a mystic as well as a practical man. He practiced the peyote rite, and "he saw things that other men do not see."[3] As a result of these visions he became the possessor of a powerful medicine. From his grandfather Momaday seems to have inherited his attitude as a survivor—do not brood over painful things in the past; make the best of what you have—as well as his keen appreciation for the spiritual side of life. Mammedaty's name became the family's surname; Mammedaty's son Alfred later changed the spelling to Momaday.

Alfred took his bride to live with his family in Mountain View, Oklahoma, the heart of Kiowa country. Shortly afterward, in February 1934, Novarro Scott Mammedaty was born at the Kiowa and Comanche Indian Hospital at Lawton, Oklahoma. The Office of Indian Affairs registered him as "⅞ degree Indian blood" and declared him an American citizen according to the act of June 2, 1924.

When Scott was six months old his parents took him to Devil's Tower, in the Black Hills of Wyoming, for a naming ceremony. Devil's Tower, or Tsoai ("Rock Tree"), as the Kiowas call it, is an igneous monolith that rises twelve hundred feet above the Belle Fourche River. The Kiowas had passed by it on their journey from their old woodland home in the north to the southern plains. Although the Kiowas moved on, Tsoai remained in their mythology as a sacred place. Pohd-lohk, Mammedaty's stepfather, named Momaday Tsoai-talee ("Rocktree Boy"). This name contributed strongly to Momaday's sense of identity as a Kiowa. Momaday describes the ceremony:

> Pohd-lohk spoke, as if telling a story, of the coming-out people, of their long journey. He spoke of how it was that everything began, of Tsoai, and of the stars falling or holding fast in strange patterns on the sky. And in this, at last, Pohd-lohk affirmed the whole life of the child in a name saying: Now you are Tsoai-talee. [P. 57]

But Momaday did not grow up among the Kiowas in Mountain View. The Mammedatys made it clear to Natachee that as an outsider she was not welcome among them. So, prodded by familial fighting and what Momaday describes as the old Kiowa wanderlust, Alfred Momaday took his family to the far Southwest.

Between 1936 and 1943 the Momadays lived on Navajo reservations in New Mexico and Arizona. Although the term

reservation has a strong pejorative connotation today, con-
juring up visions of eroded land and starving Indians, the
Momadays found the *dine bikeyeh* ("Navajo land"), to be
a place of hope and wonder:

> My parents have told me time and again what an intoxi-
> cation were those days, and I think back to them on that
> basis; they involve me in a tide of confidence and well-
> being. What on earth was not possible? I must have been
> carried along in the waves of hope and happiness that were
> gathered in the hearts of my young and free and beautiful
> parents. [Pp. 60-61]

Momaday's playmates were Navajo children. Although
Momaday always felt great admiration for the Navajos, he
was aware from an early age that he was not one of them.
As he puts it, "My peers were at removes from me, across
cultures and languages" (p. 59).

In 1943, when he was nine, the family moved to Hobbs,
New Mexico. Blacks in Hobbs lived in "Niggertown," but
Momaday mentions no other Indians, and he lived among
the whites. Boys in Hobbs were classified as toughs or
sissies, and, because Momaday was among the toughest of
the tough, he had "a stake in the dominant society" (p. 88).
The only prejudice he suffered came as a result of the resemblance he, like many Indians, bears to Orientals. Some
of his schoolmates during World War II called him a "Jap."
His own fighting ability, and that of his fellow toughs, kept
this from being a major source of irritation.

Momaday's closest friend was a young white boy named
Billy Don Johnson, and his first love was a blond-haired,
blue-eyed girl named Kathleen. His only regret about Kathleen was not that his admiration for her betrayed his own
ethnic heritage but that he never told her she was pretty.
Although he visited Oklahoma during a number of summers,
Momaday's world was the white world of Hobbs, and he
picked up some strange ideas about Indians and Indianness

as he was "formulating an idea of [himself]" (p. 97).
He transmits his childhood ideas about Indian identity
in a stream-of-consciousness passage; the questions he refers to are those of Miss Marshall, presumably his teacher:

Oh I feel so dumb I can't answer all those questions I
don't know how to be a Kiowa Indian my grandmother
lives in a house its like your house Miss Marshall or Billy
Don's house only it doesn't have lights and light switches
and the toilet is outside and you have to carry wood in
from the woodpile and water from the well but that isn't
what makes it Indian its my grandma the way she is the
way she looks her hair in braids the clothes somehow yes
the way she talks she doesn't speak English so well Scotty
you goot boy says wait I know why it's an Indian house
because there are pictures of Indians on the walls photo-
graphs of people with long braids and buckskin clothes
dresses and shirts and moccasins and necklaces and bead-
work yes that's it and there is Indian stuff all around blankets and shawls bows and arrows everyone there acts like
an Indian everyone even me and my dad when we're there
we eat meat and everyone talks Kiowa and the old people
wear Indian clothes well those dresses dark blue and braids
and hats and there is laughing Indians laugh a lot and they
sing oh yes they love to sing sometimes when an old man
comes to visit he sits in the living room and pretty soon he
just begins to sing loud with his eyes closed but really loud
and his head nodding and in the arbor there are sometimes
pretty often a lot of people and lots to eat and everyone
sings and sometimes there are drums too and it goes on
through the night that's Indian and grandma goes to Rainy
Mountain Baptist Church that's Indian and my granddad
Mammedaty is buried at Rainy Mountain and some of the
stones there have peyote pictures on them and you can hear
bobwhites there and see terrapins and scissortails and that's
Indian too. [P. 102]

It is interesting to see what Momaday the child considered
Indian—speaking faulty English, having "Indian stuff" (blan-

kets and shawls) around the house, eating meat and cat-
fish, laughing, singing, and going to the Baptist church.
There is an irony here, at the expense of the young narrator; the list shows that some of what he considers peculiarly Indian is derived from the whites—woolen blankets
and shawls, Christianity—or is common to all peoples. This,
of course, made the Baptist religion no less peculiarly Indian, for the Indians put their stamp on what they were
given, making it their own, much as the Greeks and Romans
transformed the Christianity they received from the original
Hebrew converts. Services in Rainy Mountain Baptist Church
are Indian because, although the theology is Baptist, the language of the hymns and sermon is Kiowa.

The two main points to be inferred from the passage
are, first, that Indian and white cultures have blended during the years the races have been in contact; and, second,
Scott is the first member of his father's family who has
not grown up among the Kiowas and learned to speak
their language. His ideas of his identity as an Indian are
therefore complex and ambiguous.

In 1946, when he was twelve, Momaday moved to Jemez
Pueblo, in central New Mexico, the Walatowa of *House
Made of Dawn*. His parents became teachers at the day
school, and the family lived in the school building. The
Momadays took the job at Jemez because, although they
had liked Hobbs, they missed the "old, sacred world" of
the Indians. Momaday loved the land and people of Jemez,
which he calls the "last, best home of my childhood" (p.
117). Although we have become a mobile people, Americans,
Indians and otherwise, still have a very strong sense of
place, and we feel our strongest ties to the place where
we grew up. Malcolm Cowley expresses it most poignantly
in *Exile's Return:* "Somewhere the turn of a dirt road or
the unexpected crest of a hill reveals your own childhood,
the fields where you once played barefoot, the kindly trees,
the landscape by which all others are measured and con-

20

demned."⁴ To Momaday this stretch of land is the Jemez Valley, to which he became extremely attached:

> A part of my life happened to take place at Jemez. I existed in that landscape, and then my existence was indivisible with it. I placed my shadow there in the hills, my voice in the wind that ran there, in those old mornings and afternoons and evenings. It may be that the old people there watch for me in the streets; it may be so. [P. 142]

Although he has lived in California for many years, Momaday still considers Jemez, and New Mexico in general, the place that he is from.

Jemez, as described by Momaday in *The Names* and *House Made of Dawn,* is an interesting blend of cultures. The people are Tanoan Pueblos, related distantly to the Aztecs. Jemez culture is very old, deriving from the cliff dwellers who lived above Jemez centuries ago. The Spanish conquistadors imposed Christianity on the Pueblos in the late sixteenth century, and by the time Momaday arrived in New Mexico the Tanoans had been Catholics for three hundred years. As it is depicted by Momaday in *House Made of Dawn,* the religion of the Jemez blends Christianity with their older faith: on the Feast of San Diego the Jemez carry an effigy of their patron saint through the streets, go to mass, and then dance in the kiva. The legend of Santiago as related by Momaday in *House Made of Dawn* is a combination of a saint's life and a typical Indian trickster tale.

Language and nationality are central determinants of culture. New Mexico became part of the United States in the nineteenth century, and, although it retains its Spanish flavor, the principal language is of course English. So, when the Momadays of *The Names* arrive at Jemez in the 1940s, they find a Pueblo village, in which the religion is a blend of Spanish Catholicism and Tanoan beliefs. In this Jemez setting Scott's English-speaking Kiowa and Cherokee parents teach young Scott and the other boys what the world

21

is like and what it means to be an American. Small wonder that Momaday's ideas of his ethnic identity are complex. But whatever the strands that went into Jemez culture, the Jemez were at home in it. And however much Momaday loved the land and people, in a sense he and his family were outsiders. He tells us in *The Names:*

> Throughout the year there were ceremonies of many kinds, and some of these were secret dances, and on these holiest days guards were posted on the roads and no one was permitted to enter the village. My parents and I kept then to ourselves, to our reservation of the day school, and in this way, through the tender of our respect and our belief, we earned the trust of the Jemez people, and were at home there. [P. 147]

Momaday's complex and ambivalent ideas about himself are reflected in his fantasies. A recurrent one first emerges while he is visiting Oklahoma, during the time when the family still lived "on the Navajo":

> Well anyway I have this gun this real-looking gun black and brown smooth and hard a carbine tomorrow I will shoot an Indian down by the creek he will see me but I will see him first and I will wait until he sees me it has to be that way of course he sees me and of course he is surprised his eyes are big and his mouth is open and he is ugly of course he has a knife it is a great big knife and it gleams and flashes in the sunlight it was stolen of course oh I know that good knife it was stolen from my grandfather one night when he left it outside by the arbor where he liked to cut meat he talked about it of course he meant to give it to my father and my father meant to give it to me it is really my knife the ugly Indian sees me and I am looking right at him and I have been looking right at him for a long time he recognizes me of course it has to be that way he has been afraid of me all these years running and hiding from me and now it has come to this he is famous because of the knife and he is called Knife sometimes Big

Knife sometimes Knife Thrower then after a moment he smiles and he is even uglier so it is you at last he says and I nod there is a moment between us then he makes his lightning move and the knife is wheeling in the air and of course I shoot him and nimbly nimbly I catch the knife in the stock of my gun over my heart and the ugly Indian staggers and slumps and pitches headfirst into a ravine and I say you're dead and of course it is so. [P. 76]

It is obvious that, even before moving to Hobbs, when most of his playmates were Navajo, there are times when Momaday thinks of Indians as alien. Knife Thrower is dangerous, and he is ugly.

In Hobbs, Momaday has fantasies in which he refers to himself as Indian—in one he calls himself Chief—but is doing things in the white world, playing football at Notre Dame, flying missions against the Japanese. Fantasies in which Indians are hostile continue at Jemez, even though there, as on the Navajo, he is very fond of the local Indians. One of these fantasies is recorded in *The Strange and True Story of My Life with Billy the Kid,* a work that was serialized in the *Santa Fe New Mexican.*[5]

Riding is an exercise of the mind. I dreamed a good deal on the back of my horse, going out into the hills alone. Desperadoes were everywhere in the brush. More than once I came upon roving bands of hostile Indians and had, on the spur of the moment, to put down an uprising. Now and then, I found a wagon train in trouble, and always among the settlers there was a lovely young girl from Charleston or Philadelphia who needed simply and more than anything else in the world to be saved. I saved her.

In this fantasy, obviously, as in that of Knife Thrower, Indians are strange and dangerous, and Momaday must fight them. These fantasies represent only part of a complex outlook, however, and they must be balanced with other statements like the one he made about the sense of his heritage that his father imparted to him: "My father told me the old Kiowa tales. These were many times more exciting than anything I found at school; they, more than the grammars and arithmetics, nourished the life of my mind." [P. 88]

But the question of who he was perplexed Momaday throughout his youth. It was the impetus for the pilgrimage he made in the mid-1960s, and for the book he wrote about it, *The Way to Rainy Mountain.*

The Way to Rainy Mountain is an informal and highly selective account of the Kiowas as they migrated from their old Rocky Mountain home in what is now Montana to the plains of present-day western Oklahoma. Momaday followed the route of the Kiowas, starting at the headwaters of the Yellowstone River and ending at his grandmother's grave at Rainy Mountain Cemetery, near Mountain View, Oklahoma.

Various sections of the book appeared in separate publications. Momaday assembled it in its present form. He published the prologue and several of the myths as *The Journey of Tai-me* in 1967. The introduction first appeared in the *Reporter* in 1967, and later as part of Tosamah's life story in *House Made of Dawn* in 1968. Momaday published the book as a whole in 1969.

In its present form the book is divided into three sections, each dealing with a different phase of the Kiowa experience: "The Setting Out," "The Going On," and "The Closing In." These sections are in turn divided into short chapters, each of which has three parts: a legend or story, a historical anecdote or observation, and a personal reminiscence. Alternating between these three types of narrative, as Kenneth Fields[6] has noted, allows Momaday, in his short book, to achieve a density and concentration approaching that of poetry.

Fields also gives a perceptive analysis of Momaday's use of a different voice for each segment. For the legends and stories Momaday uses a colloquial tone appropriate to oral delivery: "You know, everything had to begin, and this is how it was: the Kiowas came one by one into the world through a hollow log" (p. 17). The historical sections are more formal—a "tone of authority" is Fields's phrase, and Momaday often refers to the work of the anthropologist James E. Mooney.[7]

Fields describes the personal sections as "elegiac," conveying a "sense of loss." This tone is present at times, but certainly not always. I prefer the term *lyric* to describe the poetic and emotional nature of these selections, which should not be limited to any one of their many moods. Momaday generally prefers not to dwell on what he refers to as the "mean and ordinary agonies of human history," and often his mood is idyllic:

I have walked in a mountain meadow bright with Indian paintbrush, lupine, and wild buckwheat, and I have seen high in the branches of a lodgepole pine the male pine grosbeak, round and rose-colored, its dark, striped wings nearly invisible in the soft, mottled light. And the uppermost branches of the tree seemed very slowly to ride across the blue sky. [P. 23]

There is no sense of loss here, only an appreciation of that which remains. An even more remarkable example of the same attitude of making the best of what one has rather than lamenting what one has lost, an attitude Momaday ascribes to Mammedaty as well as his parents, can be seen in the personal section of chapter 16. All three sections of this chapter deal with the buffalo. Momaday has written elsewhere about his "deep, ethnic respect for this creature, the buffalo. It holds a special place in my heritage, my racial memory, and so I care about it. . . . I am concerned that it should survive."[8]

Obviously Momaday is aware that the vast herds of buffalo are gone, and that only a few small herds now remain in parks in the West. If there is anything he should feel elegiac about, it is the diminution of herds, and the captivity of the few buffalo that remain. But although the historical section is a depressing account of two old Indians on workhorses chasing a broken-down buffalo for the amusement of the townspeople of Carnegie, Oklahoma, years ago, the personal section is not only lyric, but lyrical:

> One morning my father and I walked in Medicine Park, on the edge of a small herd of buffalo. It was late in the spring, and many of the cows had newborn calves. Nearby a calf lay in the tall grass; it was red-orange in color, delicately beautiful with new life. We approached, but suddenly the cow was there in our way, her great dark head low and fearful-looking. Then she came at us, and we turned and ran as hard as we could. She gave up after a short run, and I think we had not been in any real danger. But the spring morning was deep and beautiful and our hearts were beating fast and we knew just then what it was to be alive. [P. 54]

To show the relationship of the three voices, as well as to discuss an important theme in the book, let us look at chapter 8. The legend tells of twin boys, children of the sun, who are captured by a giant who lives in a cave. The giant has been killing captives by building fires that fill the cave with smoke. But the twins had been taught a charm by their grandmother. When the smoke filled the cave they repeated *thain-mom* ("above my eyes") and the smoke remained above their eyes, where it could not suffocate them. The giant was frightened and let them go. The historical section explains the significance of the myth: "A word has power in and of itself. . . . By means of words can a man deal with the world on equal terms" (p. 42).

In the personal section Momaday tells of his grandmother Aho's use of the word *zei-dl-bei*, the word with which Aho "confronted evil and the incomprehensible" (p. 43). Momaday translates *zei-dl-bei* as "frightful," but this is a pale version of the Kiowa term, which has more the force of the French "formidable." As Momaday says, the term "was not an exclamation so much, I think, as it was a warding off, an exertion of language upon ignorance and disorder" (p. 43).

In chapter 8 the myth exemplifies the power of the word, the historical section comments on the subject of word power, and the personal section ties it to Momaday's own experience. The sacred power of the word is one of Momaday's favorite themes. In *House Made of Dawn* Tosamah— that fascinating character who bears an uncanny resemblance to Momaday, and who delivers the narrative that also serves as the introduction to *The Way to Rainy Mountain*—says of his grandmother, "Consider for a moment that old Kiowa woman, whose use of language was confined to speech, and be assured that her regard for words was always keen in proportion that she depended upon them. You see, for her words were medicine; they were magic and invisible."[9]

This is an old belief traditional to most Indians, not just Kiowas. To Indians words are a source of magical power, a key to the supernatural. As Momaday's mother Natachee puts it, "the Indian has always used words with reverence and awe, weaving them into chants and songs to create beauty and to express his daily needs and aspirations."[10] These songs not only concern earthly needs, they are a link with the supernatural, a way of obtaining power. A. Grove Day writes that "song [is] a way of tapping this superhuman force . . . the good creative principle in the world."[11]

The Indian reverence for the word combines in Momaday with the poet's reverence for the word. Through both the Kiowas and the Jemez, Momaday is familiar with Indian forms of Christianity, and he is particularly attracted to the Gospel of John because John equates the word with God: "In the beginning was the Word, and the Word was with God, and the Word was God." This passage is the text for Tosamah's sermon in *House Made of Dawn*, a sermon entitled "The Way to Rainy Mountain." According to John, God as Word creates the universe, makes something out of nothingness. Similarly, humans use words to bring order out of chaos—by thought, by speech, and by poetry.

In one sense *The Way to Rainy Mountain* is a testament to the power of the word, and to the Indian oral tradition. That "actions speak louder than words" is a precept common among white Americans, but to Indians actions can be a prelude to the word, and the words are as important in their way as actions. The Kiowas' journey from the Yellowstone to Rainy Mountain was important because on the way the tribe developed an idea of who they were as a people—they were able through words to imagine an identity in their existential act of self-creation. Who they are has changed; their old life as hunters is gone, and they are now for the most part simply Oklahomans with an exotic history. But as long as the story of the journey is told, they exist as a distinct people and culture.

> In one sense, then, *The Way to Rainy Mountain* is preeminently the history of an idea, man's idea of himself, and it has old and essential being in language. The verbal tradition by which it has been preserved has suffered a deterioration in time. What remains is fragmentary; mythology, legend, lore, and hearsay—and of course the idea itself, as crucial and complete as it ever was. That is the miracle. The journey herein recalled continues to be made anew each time the miracle comes to mind, for that is peculiarly the right and responsibility of the imagination. [P. 4]

To Momaday, telling the story of the way to Rainy Mountain is as important as making the journey was in the first place.

Another extremely important motif in the book is the relationship between the Kiowas and the horse. If they imagined their identity as lordly hunters and fighters as an existential act, it was the horse that allowed them to achieve this identity. Momaday again quotes the anthropologist Mooney on this point:

> It is unnecessary to dilate on the revolution made in the life of the Indian by the possession of the horse. Without it he was a half-starved skulker in the timber, creeping up on foot towards the unwary deer or building a brush corral with infinite labor to surround a herd of antelope, and seldom venturing more than a few days journey from home. With the horse he was transformed into the daring buffalo hunter, able to procure in a single day enough food to supply his family for a year, leaving him free then to sweep the plains with his war parties along a range of a thousand miles. [P. 61]

Momaday tells a number of stories about horses, one of the most interesting of which is about a horse who died of shame at his owner's cowardice:

> Once there was a man who owned a fine hunting horse. It was black and fast and afraid of nothing. When it was turned upon an enemy it charged in a straight line and struck at full speed; the man need have no hand upon the rein. But, you know, that man knew fear. Once during a charge he turned that animal from its course. That was a bad thing. The hunting horse died of shame. [P. 70]

The point of the story is the standard that the horse set for men. The horse, a part of nature and the natural order, was instinctively noble; people make themselves courageous by their existential choices.

To a society that depended on horses, the death or loss of a horse was a serious thing. Momaday includes one vignette about a stolen horse:

> In the winter of 1852-53, a Pawnee boy who had been held as captive among the Kiowas succeeded in running away.

29

He took with him an especially fine hunting horse, known far and wide as *Guadal-tseyu*, "Little Red." That was the most important event of the winter. The loss of that horse was a hard thing to bear. [P. 76]

It is interesting to note that what the Kiowas regarded as a tragedy would be, from another point of view, a stirring story of heroism on the part of the captive. In *The Names* Momaday tells the story again, remarking that "It might have been a different story among the Pawnees, the story of a boy." But from the point of view of his godfather, Pohd-lohk, who told him the story:

It was a tragic story—nearly as much so from his point of view as was that of the plague, which he imagined no more vividly—inasmuch as it centered upon a whole and crucial deprivation, the loss of a horse, a hunting horse, a loss that involved the very life's blood of the culture. [P. 50]

The disappearance of the buffalo and the closing in of the cavalry meant the end of the old way of life for the Kiowas, and, along with everything else they held sacred, they lost their horses. Momaday sees as a poignant symbol of this ending the cavalry's massacre of the Kiowas' horses:

After the fight at Palo Duro canyon, the Kiowas came in, a few at a time, to surrender at Fort Sill. Their horses and weapons were confiscated, and they were imprisoned. In a field just west of the post, the Indian ponies were destroyed. Nearly 800 horses were killed outright; two thousand more were sold, stolen, given away. [P. 67]

This is the most painful moment in the book.

But Momaday does not dwell on painful moments; he is more interested in the glory of the Kiowas than in their sorrows, and he prizes what he can appropriate for himself of their legacy. He himself loved to ride, and as part of the same chapter in which he tells of the slaughter of the Kiowa

30

horses he tells of his own experiences on horseback:

> In New Mexico the land is made of many colors. When I was a boy I rode out over the red and yellow and purple earth to the west of Jemez Pueblo. My horse was a small red roan, fast and easy-riding. I rode among the dunes, along the bases of mesas and cliffs, into canyons and arroyos. I came to know that country, not in the way a traveller knows the landmarks he sees in the distances, but more truly and intimately, in every season, from a thousand points of view. I know the living motion of a horse, and the sound of hooves. I know what it is, on a hot day in August or September, to ride into a bank of cold, fresh rain. [P. 67]

This, then, is Momaday's experience among the Kiowas, Navajos, and Tanoans. Next I will discuss his life in the American intellectual community, and how it shaped his works.

Chapter 3

POST-SYMBOLISM AND PROSE POEMS:

MOMADAY'S POETRY

AFTER HE HAD exhausted reservation schools, Momaday spent his last year of high school at a military school in Virginia and then enrolled in the University of New Mexico. It was there that he began writing poetry, and in 1959 published his first poem, "Earth and I Give You Turquoise," in the *New Mexico Quarterly*. After college Momaday tried a year of law school in the University of Virginia but decided that he did not like it.

When Momaday submitted some poems to a creative writing contest sponsored by Stanford University, Yvor Winters, who judged the poetry entries, awarded Momaday a graduate scholarship to Stanford and took him under his wing. Winters was a distinguished poet, famous for his powerful personality as well as for his scholarship and criticism, and he exercised an enormous influence on Momaday's verse. Winters died in 1968, and Momaday is now experimenting with new forms that Winters probably would have taken a dim view of, but his influence is still evident in much of Momaday's work.

Winters was a great whale of a man, imposing both intellectually and physically, with very marked ideas and a decidedly contentious disposition. His major scholarship was the championing of poets whose work, though excellent, had fallen into obscurity. Among his favorites were Barnabe Googe, Fulke Greville, Jones Very, and Frederick Goddard Tuckerman. None of these names are household words today, of course, but their poetry is worth reading, and, thanks to Winters's attentions, it has been republished recently. In fact, Momaday put together an edition of Tuckerman's works for his dissertation at Stanford.[1]

Along with his habit of heralding the obscure, Winters

had a way of dismissing the famous. He viewed the works of Wordsworth, Keats, Poe, and Whitman with contempt. All this may make Winters sound like a crank, but he was a very sound scholar and a brilliant teacher, and those who knew him never ignored or slighted his opinions. Momaday was very fond of Winters, although, as he admits now, his affection was mixed with awe. Winters, for his part, was endlessly impressed with Momaday. Winters was not one to understate, and after Momaday left Stanford, Winters used to tell students that not only was Scott a great poet and scholar, but he was also powerful enough to pull down the pillars of the building in which they were sitting.

Momaday earned his Ph.D. in English at Stanford and has taught English and comparative literature in the University of California (both Santa Barbara and Berkeley) and at Stanford, and is now teaching at the University of Arizona.

Winters meticulously taught Momaday the poet's craft. He introduced Momaday to a kind of poetry that Winters called post-symbolist, and under Winters's tutelage Momaday adopted post-symbolist methods.

The poets Winters identifies as post-symbolists are a diverse lot, starting with Frederick Goddard Tuckerman and Emily Dickinson, and including Wallace Stevens, Louise Bogan, Edgar Bowers, and Winters himself.[2] As Winters was well aware, the post-symbolists were in no sense a group. He makes clear that Tuckerman and Dickinson, who lived only a few miles apart in Massachusetts, neither knew, nor were influenced by, each other and certainly never thought of themselves as part of a movement. In fact, Winters makes no case for the influence of any of the post-symbolists on any of the others.

What the post-symbolists have in common is the use of imagery in such a way that descriptions of sensory details are charged with abstract meaning. Winters argues that in traditional European poetry, before the symbolists, imagery was primarily ornamental. Donne, for instance, used meta-

35

phor to illustrate a clearly stated theme. "The vehicles are more interesting than the tenor," Winters wrote, "therefore they are ornaments, and the tenor—the essential theme—suffers."³ With the symbolists, image and sensory description largely replace abstract meaning. Symbolist poetry cannot be paraphrased or reduced to rational meaning; meaning, such as it is, resides in the feeling and tone of the poem. Mallarmé, Rimbaud, and Verlaine are among the writers whose poems disassociate sense perception and feeling from conceptual understanding.⁴ In post-symbolist poetry, according to Winters, "the sharp sensory detail contained in a poem or passage is of such a nature that the detail is charged with meaning without our being told of the meaning explicitly, or is described in language indicating such meaning indirectly but clearly."⁵ Let us consider Momaday's "Angle of Geese" to see how a post-symbolist merges abstract meaning and sensory detail:

How shall we adorn
Recognition with our speech?—
Now the dead firstborn
Will lag in the wake of words.

Custom intervenes;
We are civil, something more:
More than language means,
The mute presence mulls and marks.

Almost of a mind,
We take measure of the loss;
I am slow to find
The mere margin of repose.

And one November
It was longer in the watch,
as if forever,
Of the huge ancestral goose.

So much symmetry!
Like the pale angle of time

36

                    And eternity.
        The great shape labored and fell.

                Quit of hope and hurt,
                It held a motionless gaze,
                Wide of time, alert,
        On the dark distant flurry.[6]

The poem is difficult to understand until we know more
about the circumstances Momaday is describing. The first
three stanzas are his reflections on the death of a friend's
child, and describe the inadequacy of language to encompass
such grief. The last three stanzas turn to an incident that
happened on a hunting trip Momaday took as a teenager:
he had retrieved a goose that one of the hunters had shot
and was holding it as it died. In the lines "How shall we
adorn / Recognition with our speech?" Momaday indicates,
by his choice of the verb *adorn*, that language functions
in this painful situation merely as decoration. He is alluding
to the poverty of words that one always feels in our culture
at such times. Very few Americans say, "I'm sorry your
little boy is dead"; it sounds so pitifully inadequate. They
usually use some periphrasis—"I'm sorry to hear the news"—
hoping by vagueness to imply something more meaningful.
But the idea here is that, whatever is said, the "Dead firstborn / Will lag in the wake of words."
    It is important to remember Momaday's roots in Indian
culture in reading the poem. When he says "We are civil,"
one should be aware of the connotation of *civilized* and
should contrast the traditional Indian custom of keening
the tremolo, cutting off one's hair, and even occasionally a
finger, in wild lamentation, with the "civilized" Anglo's custom of repressing grief. Indian mourning is a violent release
and purgation of grief. Accompanied by the passionate emotions of the Indian mourning ceremonies, words would have
more force. "I am sorry that your child is dead," would not
have a hollow ring in an Indian context. The context of

"Angle of Geese," however, is Anglo-Saxon America, and in taking "measure of the loss," Momaday is "slow to find / The mere margin of repose," the way to come to grips with the event emotionally. He cannot even find the margin, the edge, or beginning, of repose.

In the second half of the poem Momaday shifts without transition from the dead child to the dying goose. The link between the two is associational, to use one of Winters's favorite terms. The doctrine of association can be traced to Hobbes and Locke, who argued that ideas arise from association of sensory perceptions. The literary application of this idea affected poetic structure by replacing the traditional logical construction of poems with what Winters called "the structure of revery," and it brought about the post-symbolist practice of expressing ideas through images, which are a verbal record of sensory impressions.

In "Angle of Geese" Momaday moves in memory from the dead child of the present to the dying goose of his childhood. Momaday has described the incident at length in a column he wrote in the *Santa Fe New Mexican*.[7] His account is beautifully written, and seems worth reprinting in toto, both for its own sake and for its help in explaining the poem. It also shows the work of compression that Momaday has done in turning the childhood incident into poetry.

One of the Wild Beautiful Creatures

That day the sun never did come out. It was a strange, indefinite illumination, almost obscure, set very deep in the sky,—a heavy, humid cold without wind. Flurries of snow moved down from the mountains, one after another, and clouds of swirling mist spilled slowly down the slopes splashing in slow, slow motion on the plain.

For days I had seen migrating birds. They moved down the long corridor of the valley, keeping to the river. The day before I had seen a flock of twenty or thirty geese descend into the willows a mile or more downstream. They were still there, as far as I knew.

38

I was thirteen or fourteen years old, I suppose. I had a different view of hunting in those days, an exalted view, which was natural enough, given my situation. I had grown up in mountain and desert country, always in touch with the wilderness, and I took it all for granted. The men of my acquaintance were hunters. Indeed they were deeply committed to a hunting tradition. And I admired them in precisely those terms.

We drew near the river and began to creep, the way a cat creeps upon a sparrow. I remember that I placed my feet very carefully, one after the other, in the snow without sound. I felt an excitement welling up within me. Before us was a rise which now we were using as a blind. Beyond and below it was the river, which we could not yet see, except where it reached away at either end of our view, curving away into the pale, winter landscape. We advanced up the shallow slope, crouching, leaned into the snow and raised ourselves up on our toes in order to see. The geese were there, motionless on the water, riding like decoys. But though they were still they were not calm. I could sense their wariness, the tension that was holding them in that stiff, tentative attitude of alert.

And suddenly they exploded from the water. They became a terrible, clamorous swarm, struggling to gain their element. Their great bodies, trailing water, seemed to heave under the wild, beating wings. They disintegrated into a blur of commotion, panic. There was a deafening roar; my heart was beating like the wings of the geese.

And just as suddenly out of this apparent chaos there emerged a perfect fluent symmetry. The geese assembled on the cold air, even as the river was still crumpled with their going, and formed a bright angle on the distance. Nothing could have been more beautiful, more wonderfully realized upon the vision of a single moment. Such beauty is inspirational in itself; for it exists for its own sake.

One of the wild, beautiful creatures remained in the river, mortally wounded, its side perforated with buckshot. I waded out into the hard, icy undercurrent and took it up in my arm. The living weight of it was very great, and with its life's blood it warmed my frozen hands. I carried it for a long time. There was no longer any fear in its eyes, only something like sadness and yearning, until at last the eyes curdled in death. The great shape seemed perceptibly lighter, diminished in my hold, as if the ghost given up had gone at last to take its place in that pale angle in the long distance.

These words, like the poem, were written long after the event, after Momaday had undergone a change from an unquestioning, romantic acceptance of hunting to a viewpoint which, the reader can infer, is more critical. What remains in his mind as an adult is a memory of the pathos of the dying goose, yearning to take its place in the "bright angle" with the rest of the flock.

The poem is post-symbolist in technique because Momaday imbues his childhood experience with an abstract significance. The goose becomes the "huge ancestral goose," a prototype of geese, rather than one bird. Momaday compares the formation of the flock in flight to the angle of time and eternity, imbuing their flight with a metaphysical or transcendental dimension. The wounded goose, between life and death, is still alive and alert, and yet it is "wide of time"; that is, its impending death has released it from the bondage of time.

Using post-symbolist technique, Momaday implies a meaning in his description of the scene, though never implicitly stating it. Put baldly, the meaning is that death is not something to be dreaded but a means of escaping the trammels of time. This formulation is oversimple, only a portion of the statement that the description makes, but it does inhere in and is at the center of it. Post-symbolist images cannot be very satisfactorily reduced to prose, yet the prose element, the tenor, is definitely a crucial part of them.

"Angle of Geese" is written in syllabic verse, rather than in the accentual syllabic verse of most traditional poetry. In a syllabic line the "accented syllables must vary sufficiently in number and position that they do not follow a pattern (a pattern would give us standard meter) but must still contribute to the rhythm," whereas accentual syllabic verse contains a regular alternation of stressed and unstressed syllables.[8] In "Angle of Geese" the first and third lines of each stanza contain five syllables and the second and fourth lines contain seven. The rhythm of the poem is very subtle, and its effect not markedly different from that of prose, even though the first and third lines of each stanza rhyme. Since the rhymed lines are not usually heavily endstopped, they are not at all obtrusive and, indeed, might even escape the notice of a casual reader.

The poem recalls Winters in its solemn tone and stately rhythm, in its curiously formal and abstract diction, and in its fondness for polysyllabic, latinate words. "How shall we adorn / Recognition with our speech?" is reminiscent of some of Winters's verse, for instance:

> Amid the walls' insensate white, some crime
> Is redefined above the sunken mass
> Of crumbled years; logic reclaims the crass,
> Frees from historic dross the invidious mime.[9]

The rhyme is heavier, the meter iambic pentameter, but, as in Momaday's poem, the diction is formal, the language abstract and latinate.

Winters was considered an academic poet, and in Momaday's early verse we can sometimes get a faint whiff of the lamp. Consider, for instance, "The Bear."

> What ruse of vision,
> escarping the wall of leaves,
> rending incision
> into countless surfaces,
>
> would cull and color
> his somnolence, whose old age
> has outworn valor,
> all but the fact of courage?

> Seen, he does not come,
> move, but seems forever there,
> dimensionless, dumb,
> in the windless noon's hot glare.
>
> More scarred than others
> these years since the trap maimed him,
> pain slants his withers,
> drawing up the crooked limb.
>
> Then he is gone, whole,
> without urgency, from sight,
> as buzzards control,
> imperceptibly, their flight.[10]

The reader might naturally suppose that a poem by an Indian about a bear has been inspired by a hunting incident, but, as it happens, the model for this bear is Old Ben in Faulkner's "The Bear."[11] Momaday not only depicts the same scene as Faulkner—the confrontation of the hunter and the huge, old bear—but he borrows from Faulkner's diction as well:

> Then he saw the bear. It did not emerge, appear: it was just there, immobile, fixed in the green and windless noon's hot dappling, not as big as he had dreamed it but as big as he had expected, bigger, dimensionless against the dappled obscurity, looking at him.[12]

Momaday uses Faulkner's passage the way Shakespeare uses Plutarch's description of Cleopatra's barge, borrowing the most vivid phrases, preserving the essence of the description, and transmuting prose into poetry. Like "Angle of Geese," "The Bear" is syllabic verse, lines one and three of each stanza having five syllables, and lines two and four having seven. Momaday makes greater use of rhyme here than in "Angle of Geese," with alternating lines rhyming. Still, there is not much endstopping or heavy stress on final syllables, so the rhyme is unobtrusive.

Winters had commented that the language of the poem

is very quiet, and "could well be the language of distinguished prose."[13] He concludes that it is poetry "by virtue of the careful selection of details and the careful juxtaposition of these details, selection and juxtaposition which result in concentration of meaning, and by virtue of its rhythm, which is the rhythm of verse, but very subtle."[14] This is exaggerated, since the language of prose never includes rhyme, but it is worth noting because it indicates that, even at its most formal, Momaday's poetry was not that far from his recent prose poetry, although at first the new poems seem a dramatic departure.

The importance of noting that Faulkner's Ben and not some real bear provided the model for Momaday's poem is that it reminds the reader that Momaday is a man of letters, not a noble savage, and that his poetry is in the same literary tradition as that of any American writing today. But "The Bear" is not only literary; like most of Momaday's verse, it is vividly descriptive. More than anything else Winters detested vagueness, and inveighed against it to Momaday and all his other students. Winter's argument with the romantics was that they seldom described poetic subjects in visual terms.[15]

Shelley was one of Winters' favorite examples of this romantic tendency, because his famous poem "The Skylark" is a series of similes, none of which serve to describe the bird in its avian manifestation. In the poem Shelley compares the lark to a "cloud of fire," a "poet hidden," a "highborn maiden," and an "unbodied joy." In contrast, Momaday presents the bear, not in full detail, but in a few descriptive strokes, as in a line drawing that suggests as much as it depicts, but nonetheless presents a fully realized creature. We see, or sense, the bear—massive, old, still, and maimed.

Momaday's bear, however, is no less a symbol than Shelley's lark. To Faulkner, Old Ben was not only a bear, but also a symbol of the vanishing wilderness. Momaday incorporates a sense of this into his poem. As Winters describes it, "The poem is more descriptive than anything else, yet in the third and last stanzas the details are more than physical and indicate something of the essential wilderness."[16] Momaday is careful to soften the effect by the use of "seems," but the bear, "dimensionless, . . . forever there," is clearly more than one particular animal; he is also the incarnation of some primeval, fundamental truth about the wilderness.

Another poem in which Momaday combines symbols with minute and keen description is "Buteo Regalis":

> His frailty discrete, the rodent turns, looks.
> What sense first warns? The winging is unheard,
> Unseen but as distant motion made whole,
> Singular, slow, unbroken in its glide.
> It veers, and veering, tilts broad-surfaced wings.
> Aligned, the span bends to begin the dive
> And falls, alternately white and russet,
> Angle and curve, gathering momentum.[17]

Here is a brief sketch of a hawk swooping to its kill. The prey is an unspecified rodent; we are not told whether it is a rat, mouse, or prairie dog. Momaday alternates the use of syllabic verse with iambic pentameter (lines 2, 4, 5, and 6 are iambic), and Winters suggests, persuasively, that "the first and third lines, in their syllabic rhythm suggest the sudden hesitation; the four pentameter lines suggest the smooth motion of the soaring hawk; the last two lines in their syllabic rhythm and fragmented phrasing, suggest the rapid and confusing descent."[18]

Notice Momaday's description of the rodent: its frailty is "discrete"—separate—a reference to its isolation in its last moments of life. Momaday depicts the hawk impressionistically. The rodent senses it more than sees it—"Unseen but as a distant motion made whole." The vignette is not completed—Momaday does not tell us whether the hawk gets his prey or not. Somehow the outcome seems less important than the iconic glimpse we get: hawk stooping, rodent turning. It is a glimpse into the wild heart of nature. As Winters puts it, "It seems rather a perception of the 'discrete' wilderness, the essential wilderness."

After Winters, the most important influence on Momaday's early poetry was the work of Frederick Goddard Tuckerman, the nineteenth-century New Englander whose poems were the subject of Momaday's Ph.D. dissertation at Stanford. Momaday's interest in Tuckerman persisted beyond his dissertation. He wrote an article on Tuckermans' "The Cricket," published an edition of Tuckerman's poems, and still includes Tuckerman in his course on the antiromantic movement in nineteenth-century American literature.

There are some notable parallels between Momaday and Tuckerman. Tuckerman, the earliest of the post-symbolists, wrote poetry that combined subtle and detailed descriptions of nature with symbolism, a practice Momaday has emulated. Momaday, like Tuckerman before him, is an amateur naturalist. Furthermore, both men studied but never practiced the law, preferring to become poets.

Tuckerman influenced Momaday both stylistically and philosophically. Stylistically, Momaday admired and adopted Tuckerman's naturalist's eye for detail. Tuckerman's poems are full of references to flowers like bloodroot, king orchis, pearlwort, and jacinth, and herbs like wastebalm and feverfew. Sometimes Tuckerman just names the plants; sometimes, in his best verse, he describes them, briefly but vividly. Momaday describes Tuckerman's poems as "remarkable, point-blank descriptions of nature; they are filled with small, precise, and whole things: purring bees and varvain spikes, shives and amaryllis, wind flowers and stramony."[19] The impression one has of Tuckerman is of a man who sees the world of nature clearly and distinctly, rather than through a romantic blur.

But Tuckerman is just as capable as Shelley of making

a creature into a symbol. In "The Cricket," which in Momaday's opinion is Tuckerman's greatest poem,[20] the cricket
is a complex figure symbolizing the forces of nature. Tuckerman asserts that to understand the cricket's song is to understand the universe, an idea akin to Tennyson's statement in
"Flower in the Crannied Wall."[21] Tuckerman concludes that
it is an immoral act to pry into nature's secrets, what Chaucer
called "Goddes pryvetee." Although Tuckerman does not
make the comparison, he apparently sees the invasion of
the natural world by the probing mind as similar to the
original sin of eating of the tree of knowledge. Tuckerman's
conclusion is existential; the universe is impenetrable, and
the important question, as Momaday put it in his article
on "The Cricket," is "how to live in the certainty of death."[22]

Philosphically, although it would be too simplistic to
attribute Momaday's existential views solely to Tuckerman's
influence, it is worth noting that the men share a similar
outlook. Momaday's poem "Before an Old Painting of the
Crucifixion" is informed by ideas very similar to those of
"The Cricket":

I ponder how He died, despairing once.
I've heard the cry subside in vacant skies,
In clearings where no other was. Despair,
Which, in the vibrant wake of utterance,
Resides in desolate calm, preoccupies,
Though it is still. There is no solace there.

That calm inhabits wilderness, the sea,
And where no peace inheres but solitude;
Near death it most impends. It was for Him,
Absurd and public in His agony,
Inscrutably itself, nor misconstrued,
Nor metaphrased in art or pseudonym:

A vague contagion. Old, the mural fades . . .
Reminded of the fainter sea I scanned,
I recollect: How mute in constancy!

I could not leave the wall of palisades
Till cormorants returned my eyes on land.
The mural but implies eternity:

Not death, but silence after death is change.
Judean hills, the endless afternoon,
The farther groves and arbors seasonless
But fix the mind within the moment's range.
Where evening would obscure our sorrow soon,
There shines too much a sterile loveliness.

No imprecisions of commingled shade,
No shimmering deceptions of the sun,
Herein no semblances remark the cold
Unhindered swell of time, for time is stayed
The Passion wanes into oblivion,
And time and timelessness confuse, I'm told.

These centuries removed from either fact
Have lain upon the critical expanse
And been of little consequence. The void
Is calendared in stone; the human act,
Outrageous, is in vain. The hours advance
Like flecks of foam borne landward and destroyed.[23]

Like W. H. Auden's "Musée des Beaux Arts," this poem is about a poet's reaction to a painting, and his consequent reflections about life. From the outset it is apparent that Momaday takes an existential view of the crucifixion: God is dead. Christ dies in despair, his cry subsiding in "vacant skies"—skies empty of God. Man is alone on earth, "where no peace inheres but solitude." To Momaday, Christ's agony is absurd and inscrutable, or it has meaning only as a singular gesture; it did not, as Christianity teaches, bring redemption to man. Christ's death is often misconstrued, Momaday says, or translated into art, into pictures like the mural. The mural implies eternity, but there is none. The change after death is not to eternal life, but to silence, nothingness. During one's lifetime there is little comfort because time is relentless. Momaday's great image is taken from the sea he watches in the poem. "The cold / Unhindered swell of time" is a prototypical example of a post-symbolist image. Momaday expands on the image in the last stanza: "The hours advance / Like flecks of foam borne landward and destroyed."[24]

The idea that time is passing ceaselessly is of course one of the most familiar themes in poetry, the basis of *ubi sunt* and *carpe diem* poems, for example, but Momaday's lines are particularly reminiscent of the best lines in "The Cricket":

> Behold the autumn goes,
> The Shadow grows,
> The moments take hold of eternity;
> Even while we stop to wrangle or repine
> Our lives are gone
> Like thinnest mist,
> Like yon escaping colour in the trees.[25]

Momaday continues to write poems in his conservative, Wintersian mode—poems, for instance, like "Anywhere Is a Street into the Night," the title poem from the collection that he published after a trip to Russia. But he has also begun to experiment with a more fluid form, the prose poem. These are usually about Indian subjects, and although, as Winters pointed out, even his most traditional poems approached the "rhythm of stately prose," these prose poems seem a radical departure. They most resemble the oral tradition of the Indian tale, and, indeed, most of them are short narratives.

The Fear of Bo-Talee

Bo-talee rode easily among his enemies, once, twice, three— and four times. And all who saw him were amazed, for he was utterly without fear; so it seemed. But afterwards he said: Certainly I was afraid. I was afraid of the fear in the eyes of my enemies.

The Stalker

Sampt'e drew the string back and back until he felt the bow wobble in his hand, and he let the arrow go. It shot across the long light of the morning and struck the black face of a stone in the meadow; it glanced then away towards the west, limping along in the air; and then it settled down in the grass and lay still. Sampt'e approached; he looked at it with wonder and was wary; honestly he believed that the arrow might take flight again; so much of his life did he give into it.[26]

These two short recitatives might have appeared as chapters in *The Way to Rainy Mountain.* They have the stately oral cadence of the Indian teller of tales and, although strongly rhythmical, have shed the last formal regular strictures of verse.

Momaday is a fine poet, but in my opinion he is at his best in prose. His prose is masterful in *House Made of Dawn,* but it is at its best in the lyrical short passages of *The Way to Rainy Mountain* and *The Names.* These new poems, like "The Fear of Bo-talee," seem to indicate that Momaday's verse and prose, once so different, are conjoining to create a single and powerful voice. Momaday's prose, both fiction and nonfiction, had been written solely from an Indian point of view; his verse, academic and formal, showed more trace of his literary than of his ethnic beginnings. These new prose poems are Indian in tone and subject.

Chapter 4

HOUSE MADE OF DAWN

NOBODY'S PROTEST NOVEL

HOUSE MADE OF DAWN is Momaday's masterpiece. In fact, I do not think it is excessive praise to say that it is one of the best American novels of the last decade. The book received the Pulitzer Prize for literature in 1969, an indication that its merits have not been lost on the critics. Although it has been thoroughly praised, it has been less thoroughly understood.

House Made of Dawn is the story of Abel (we never learn his last name), an illegitimate son of a Tanoan mother and an unknown father, probably a Navajo. The story begins with Abel's return from World War II to his village of Walatowa, a fictionalized version of the Jemez Pueblo where Momaday grew up. Abel is so drunk when he arrives that he fails to recognize his grandfather, who has come to pick him up. Abel feels lost on his return, and obviously his problem is largely that he has lost his cultural identity.

On the Festival of Santiago, Abel enters a ceremonial game in which men on horseback attempt to pull a rooster out of the ground. The rider who accomplishes this feat is then entitled to beat another of the participants with the rooster. The winner, an albino Tanoan named Fragua, chooses to beat Abel, who is unnerved and humiliated. Several days later Abel kills the albino in a knife fight outside a bar and is sent to jail for seven years.

When Abel gets out of jail he is "relocated" in Los Angeles, where he works diligently at his job for a short period. But he is harassed by a sadistic policeman named Martinez and taunted by a Kiowa named Tosamah, who considers Abel an ignorant savage. Eventually Abel turns to drink and loses his job. In his drunkenness Abel attacks Martinez, and Martinez gives him a beating that is almost fatal. After a long, slow recovery, Abel returns to Wala-towa as his grandfather is dying. When his grandfather dies, Abel performs the traditional preburial rituals and then prepares to enter a traditional Tanoan race for good hunting and harvests that his grandfather had won years before. The book ends with Abel running, singing the words to a Navajo prayer. Apparently he has found a sort of peace of mind by joining in the cultural life of the Tanoan community.

Knowing about Momaday's experiences as a Kiowa growing up among the Navajo and Jemez is very important if we are to understand Momaday's treatment of Abel. There are also recognizable literary influences: Momaday owes a debt to writers like Faulkner for his use of stream of consciousness and limited point of view—for instance, in the scene in which Abel lies half dead on the beach after Martinez beats him. Also apparent is the influence of Melville's symbolism in the significance Momaday makes of the whiteness of the albino.

The result of these influences is a masterfully complex novel. Unfortunately, the tendency of most white American readers (at least if my students of the past ten years are any indication) is to read the book simplistically, as a protest novel. According to this reading, Abel, the Indian protagonist, is a noble red victim of the barbaric forces of white America. The impression is based on several things. First, because Momaday is himself an Indian, readers often expect him to blame Abel's failure on racial injustice. Second, Abel's name is an obvious allusion to the Bible's first victim. When I ask my students who is the Cain that destroys Abel, they always answer that it is white society. Last, if not least, there is the inevitable comparison with Ira Hayes, the Pima Indian who helped raise the flag on Iwo Jima, an act memorialized in the famous Marine Corps statue. When Hayes returned to his reservation after the war, he became an alcoholic and one evening, out of doors,

53

he passed out and died from exposure. His death received a good deal of attention from the press, and Hayes's story served as the basis of the film *The Outsider.* Tony Curtis played Hayes in accordance with the Hollywood stereotype of the Indian as victim. The point of the movie was that Indians can die for their country but cannot live in it with dignity.

Whatever the reasons for the reader to believe that Abel is simply a victim of white society, the conclusion is incorrect—far too simplistic. Momaday presents a highly complex portrait of Abel and does not rely on Hollywood clichés or on those of students.

First of all, although there is a general similarity in the situation of Abel and Ira Hayes—both are Indian veterans from the Southwest who cannot readjust to their role in postwar America, and so turn to alcohol—the resemblance may simply be coincidental. Momaday has said that his chief models in creating Abel were Indians he knew at Jemez. In an interview in November, 1974, Momaday told Charles Woodard, "I knew an Abel at Jemez who was a close neighbor. . . . I was thinking of him; he's one of the people who adds to the composite Abel."[1]

No doubt Momaday was familiar with Hayes's story, and it may have been somewhat in his mind when he created the character of Abel, but there is an enormous difference between Momaday's complex character and the stereotype into which Hollywood turned Hayes. To those who read press accounts of Hayes's death or saw *The Outsider,* Hayes was a hero during the war and a victim of white injustice afterwards. In the normal way these terms are used, Abel was neither. In a very curious, ambiguous sense, he may have been both, but in ways so different from Hayes that there is really no basis for comparison.

The only glimpse we get of Abel's combat experience is a curious scene in which Abel gives an enemy tank the finger. His fellow soldiers find this bizarre, not heroic. The gesture, totally inexplicable in terms of modern warfare, seems a rough equivalent of the old plains Indian custom of counting coups. Plains warriors considered it more glorious to ride up to an armed enemy and touch him harmlessly with a stick they called a coupstick, than to shoot him from a distance. Counting coups, which insulted the enemy by showing him that you scorned his ability to harm you, seems to be what Abel has in mind, though Momaday never says so. This is not to imply that Abel, a Navajo/Tanoan, would have known about or have consciously thought about coups; nevertheless, he is displaying the same attitude toward the enemy. Momaday, a Kiowa, would certainly know about counting coups.

The matter of Abel as victim of white injustice brings us to the next point, the significance of his name. Momaday told Woodard, "I know about Abel and the Bible and that certainly was in my mind, but I don't think I chose the name on that account." This seems a slight evasion. Momaday may have chosen the name because he knew an Abel, but he does not give Abel a surname, and a man as sensitive to symbolic meanings as Momaday could not have failed to realize that his readers would have imagined a link between a character named simply Abel and the Bible's first victim. The question is, victim of what? In these secular times, even in the Bible Belt, where I teach, students have forgotten the Bible. Cain was Abel's brother, not some hostile outsider. In *House Made of Dawn* two of the men who do the worst damage to Abel are his brother Indians, John Tosamah, the Kiowa "Priest of the Sun," who ridicules Abel until he drives him to drink (admittedly a short haul) and Juan Reyes Fragua, the Tanoan albino who humiliates Abel, and whom Abel murders, as a result spending seven years in jail. Abel's third tormentor, the sadistic policeman Martinez, is either a Chicano or an Indian with a Spanish surname—at any rate, he is not an Anglo-American. He appears to be a free-lance grafter, and not in any very direct sense a representative of the white society the students have indicted.

The albino is a very curious figure. From Fray Nicolas's letter of January 5, 1875, we know that at the time Fragua and Abel participate in the Festival of Santiago, Fragua is seventy years old, although apparently still remarkably athletic.[2] In some mysterious way the albino is evil. In the scene in which the albino watches, or spies on, Abel's grandfather Francisco, Francisco senses the presence of evil, although he sees no one. The scene is ambiguous, but it is evident that Momaday wants the reader to apprehend the albino as evil and possibly to recognize him as a witch (Indians use the term for men and women both). H. S. McAllister argues that the albino is linked through witchcraft and possession with Fray Nicolas and the Bahkyush witch Nicolas *teah-whau*. The three are, in McAllister's words, "three manifestations of a single person."[3] I find this thesis far-fetched, or at least in excess of the evidence McAllister has marshaled, but according to Momaday himself, the albino is a witch. Momaday told Woodard about the passage in question: "He [the albino] is manifesting the evil of his presence. Witchcraft and the excitement of it is part of that too." Abel is aware that the albino is evil, but his decision to kill him seems to spring from a specific incident, his beating at the Festival of Santiago.

When the albino pulls the rooster out of the ground and chooses Abel to beat, Abel is infuriated by the humiliation and determines to kill the albino. Momaday refers to this gory ritual as a game, and it is a game in the sense that it is an activity done for entertainment and governed by a well-defined set of arbitrary rules. If Abel decides to play the game, he should be aware of the risks and willing to suffer the consequences. His anger and decision to kill the albino exceed the rules of the game, and indicate a mind out of touch with its cultural context. It is as if a black

halfback, considering it a racial incident when he is tackled
by a white linebacker, wants to fight him. A man who does
not want to be knocked down should not play football,
and a man who does not want to be beaten with a rooster
should avoid participating in rituals in which that is the
practice. Nonetheless, Abel does not see it that way. He
kills the albino.

In understanding the albino we must recognize the symbolic dimension to his character. The conjunction of whiteness and evil inevitably suggests Melville's *Moby Dick*. In
chapter 42, "The Whiteness of the Whale," Melville describes
how white not only symbolizes purity and goodness to men
but also transmits the spectral qualities of terror and evil.
As Melville puts it, white is "the intensifying agent in things
the most appalling to mankind."[4] Melville particularly mentions the albino man who "so particularly repels and often
shocks the eye, as that sometimes he is loathed by his own
kith and kin."[5] Momaday told Woodard of his special interest in Melville, whom he teaches in his course on antiromantic American literature. In his interview with Woodard
he confirms the influence of Melville in the depiction of the
albino.[6]

One of the most interesting things about the albino is
that throughout *House Made of Dawn*, Momaday refers to
him as the "white man." We must remember that we are
dealing with symbolism here, not allegory. Momaday's albino does not stand for Caucasian Americans in the way
that Bunyan's Mr. Wordly Wiseman stands for earthly
knowledge. Primarily, Juan Reyes Fragua is a Tanoan Indian who interacts with other characters on a purely realistic
level. There is an additional symbolic and ironic sense,
however, in which the "white man" represents white society.
Perhaps this is most strongly apparent in the scene in which
Abel murders the albino. Although Momaday is describing
a stabbing, the terms he uses are obviously sexual:

The white man raised his arms, as if to embrace him. . . . Then he closed his hands on Abel and drew him close. Abel heard the strange excitement of the white man's breath, and the quick, uneven blowing in his ear, and felt the blue shivering lips upon him, felt even the scales of the lips and hot slippery point of the tongue, writhing. [P. 78]

What is happening here, on a literal level, is that Abel is killing the albino while, on a symbolic level, the white man is raping Abel. What exactly this means in symbolic terms is impossible to put neatly into words. Momaday has told Woodard about Fragua: "There is a kind of ambiguity that is creative in the albino—the white man, the albino, that equation, whatever it is."

Abel's other "brother" is Tosamah, the enigmatic Priest of the Sun who resembles Momaday in a number of respects. First of all, Tosamah is the only Kiowa in *House Made of Dawn*. Second, Momaday's description of Tosamah —"big, lithe as a cat, narrow eyed"—fits Momaday himself. More important, Momaday has Tosamah express some of his most deeply felt ideas about the sacred nature of the word and the power of language in the sermon Tosamah delivers to his parishoners.[7] Finally, and most remarkably, when Tosamah tells his life story, it is the story of Momaday's life. The chapter headed "January 27" in the "Priest of the Sun" section of *House Made of Dawn* is also the introduction to *The Way to Rainy Mountain*.

If Tosamah is the character in *House Made of Dawn* who most closely resembles Momaday, how do we account for the way Tosamah despises Abel? Tosamah says of Abel that the whites

deloused him and gave him a lot of free haircuts and let him fight on their side. But was he grateful? Hell, no, man. He was too damn dumb to be civilized. . . . He turned out to be a real primitive sonuvabitch, and the first time he got hold of a knife he killed a man. That must have embarrassed the hell out of them. [P. 135]

Obviously Tosamah is being ironic about the generosity of the whites—"they let him fight on their side"—but he means what he says about Abel—that he is "too damn dumb to be civilized," and "a real primitive sonuvabitch." Tosamah does not see anything noble in Abel's savagery. He is ashamed that Abel, a member of the same ethnic group, has made a spectacle of himself. Abel has "embarrassed the hell out of" Tosamah by fulfilling the white stereotype of the Indian—primitive, violent, superstitious, backward, and, significantly, dumb—inarticulate.

Tosamah is so scornful of Abel that he baits him until he breaks Abel's spirit. After Tosamah's taunts, Abel gets violently drunk and loses his job; with it go his hopes for a new life in California. Tosamah never shows any compassion or understanding of Abel; to Tosamah, Abel is simply an object of derision. Momaday's attitude toward Abel is obviously more sympathetic than Tosamah's, but it is hard to avoid the conclusion that Tosamah reflects one side of Momaday.

Recall that, during Momaday's youth, although he too was an Indian, he was an outsider among the Navajo and Jemez Indians. In his fantasy world he often saw himself as white and Indians as hostile. This side of Momaday is reflected in Tosamah.

But Tosamah is only one side of Momaday, and he is a caricature at that. Momaday gives him the middle name of Big Bluff, and Tosamah, in fact, sounds very much like the Kiowa word for "woman of the house," to·so·a·mah. Momaday says Tosamah has the voice of a "great dog," and there are deflating, comic touches in his sermon. "May the Great Spirit—can we knock off the talking back there—be with you always." In short, Tosamah reflects Momaday's self-irony, and he is clearly more of a caricature than a self-portrait of the artist. If Momaday is like Tosamah, however, he is also like Abel: both are outsiders. Although Momaday got along well with the Jemez, his accounts of early life at Jemez Pueblo make it clear that he felt he was different from the local Indians.

Abel's problems, in fact, seems to stem chiefly from the intolerance of other Indians. I do not mean just a few individuals like Tosamah and the albino, but the whole Tanoan community of Walatowa. Abel's mother and grandfather Francisco were Tanoans, but Abel was considered an outsider because of his illegitimacy: "He did not know who his father was. His father was a Navajo, they said, or a Sia, or an Isleta, an outsider anyway, which made him and his mother and Vidal somehow foreign and strange" (p. 15).

Abel's mother and brother die during his childhood, and Abel is alone in a hostile world save for his grandfather. Obviously Abel is not living successfully within the Indian cultural tradition before he goes to live in the white world, although this is the impression given on the cover of the New American Library edition—the one the students use: "His name was Abel, and he lived in two worlds. One was that of his fathers, wedding him to the rhythm of the seasons, the harsh beauty of the land, the ecstasy of the drug called peyote. The other was the world of the twentieth century, goading him into a compulsive cycle of sexual exploits, dissipation, and disgust." Abel's chief problem, both before he goes to war and immediately after he returns, is that he is *not* living in the world of his fathers. He does not know who his father is, nor does he know who he is himself.

Abel's problem is most acute just after his return from the war. He finds that he is totally alienated from his grandfather. He is frustrated because he is completely inarticulate. Language, the power of the word, is extremely important to Momaday, and he makes it clear that, because he cannot express himself, Abel is emotionally stifled and repressed, and so potentially violent.

His return to the town had been a failure, for all his looking forward. He had tried in the days that followed to speak
to his grandfather, but he could not say the things he wanted;
he had tried to pray, to sing, to enter the old rhythm of
the tongue, but he was no longer attuned to it. . . . Had
he been able to say . . . anything of his own language
. . . [it] would have once again shown him whole to himself; but he was dumb. [P. 57]

A short time later Momaday describes Abel's walk into the
hills:

He was alone, and he wanted to make a song out of the
colored canyon, the way the women of Torreón made songs
upon their looms out of colored yarn, but he had not got
the right words together. It would have been a creation
song; he would have sung slowly of the first world, of fire
and flood, and of the emergence of dawn from the hills.
[P. 57]

The song Abel is looking for is the Navajo hymn "House
Made of Dawn," which he later learns from his friend Ben-
ally.

Abel remains inarticulate and emotionally repressed
throughout his years in jail and during his relocation in
Los Angeles, where, as Momaday points out symbolically
with a scene that includes grunions (p. 83), he is like a
fish out of water. Abel achieves emotional release with the
death of his grandfather. When Francisco dies, Abel buries
him in the prescribed Tanoan fashion. For the first time
since his disastrous participation in the rooster ceremony,
Abel takes part in a Tanoan ritual. The act symbolizes his
entry into the culture of his fathers. Immediately after preparing his grandfather for burial, Abel participates in the
traditional race for good hunting and harvests. His grandfather had won this contest more than half a century earlier, in what had been the climactic point of his life: "Some

61

years afterward, when he was no longer young and his leg had been stiffened by disease, he made a pencil drawing on the first page of a ledger book which he kept with his store of prayer feathers in the rafters of his room. It was the likeness of a straight black man running in the snow" (p. 12). One cannot help thinking of the contrast between him and A. E. Housman's runner ("To an Athlete Dying Young"), who dies shortly after winning his race. Francisco survives to join the "rout / Of lads that wore their honors out, / Runners whom renown outran."

As the novel ends, Abel smears his arms and chest with ashes, as the ritual prescribes, and joins the runners, though unlike Francisco he runs behind them. As he runs, he sings the song he had longed to sing: "House made of pollen, house made of dawn."

This is a happy ending, or as happy an ending as the novel will allow. Abel has entered into the ceremonial life of his people, and he has regained his voice. His running is symbolic of his emotional and spiritual health, even though his legs buckle and he falls. For him to win the race would be impossibly corny—a totally discordant note of contrived cheerfulness.

Abel does not win this race, nor does Momaday imply that he will win in the future. Yet by the simple act of entering the race Abel establishes that, despite the on-slaughts of the Cains who have attacked him, he has survived. Abel survives because he is able to integrate himself into Tanoan culture. But this is not to say that he has rejected white culture and returned to an Indian culture. There is no such thing as a pure culture.

The culture of Walatowa is particularly complex. It was originally a Tanoan Pueblo settlement. When the Conquistadores conquered the Pueblos, they introduced the Spanish language and Catholicism; with the Mexican War, Walatowa became part of America, and a new language and culture were superimposed on the other two. For centuries the

Walatoans practiced both Christianity and their native religion, but slowly the religions merged, and by the time of the novel's central action the people of Walatowa have their own peculiar brand of Pueblo Christianity, with its own rituals and mythology. Momaday explicitly chronicles the shift. Fray Nicolas, the nineteenth-century priest who keeps a diary, reveals his horror that his sacristan Francisco (Abel's grandfather) participates in the traditional Tanoan ceremonies by dancing in the Kiva, the sacred dugout of the Pueblos. Fray Nicolas believes that practicing traditional Indian rituals is sinful and disgusting, and he expects the Holy Spirit to strike Francisco down when the boy assists at mass. By 1945 the attitude of the church apparently had changed, because the current priest, Father Olguin, proudly shows Angela St. John the ceremonial dancing and other rituals that take place on the Feast of Santiago.

In fact, the whole myth and ceremony of Santiago is an illustration of the merging of the cultures. Santiago is Momaday's name for San Diego (both are Spanish names for Saint James), the saint whose day was celebrated in Jemez on November 12.[8] The Tanoans celebrate the holiday in the novel by going to mass and then carrying an effigy of Porcingula, Our Lady of the Angels—a saint they inherited from the Bahkyush—through the streets to her position next to the kiva where

> The Lady would stand all day in her shrine, and the governor and his officials would sit in attendance at her feet, and one by one the dancers of the squash and turquoise clans would appear on top of the kiva, coming out upon the sky in their rich ceremonial dress, descend the high ladder to the earth, and kneel before her. [P. 73]

Momaday's myth of Santiago also shows the blending of the cultures, as it combines the Christian genre of the saints tale, with its miracles, and the Indian myth of origin that features the trickster as culture hero. Santiago, who

63

escapes the evil king by the miracle of the rooster and horses (which is as much trickster prank as Christian miracle), ends by providing plants and animals for the Pueblo people, the standard task of the culture-hero trickster.[9]

Like Joyce's *Finnegan's Wake*, *House Made of Dawn* ends as it begins. Abel is running and, as he runs, he sings. It is important to notice *what* he sings: the Navajo prayer song, *House Made of Dawn*. Abel has found himself in his own culture, a blend of Tanoan, Spanish, and American influences, and he is singing a Navajo song, appropriate in light of his own mixed ancestry.

Chapter 5

BLACKFEET SURREALISM

The Poetry of James Welch

Lois Welch

James Welch

JAMES WELCH is Blackfeet on his father's side (Blackfeet say "Blackfeet," not "Blackfoot"), and Gros Ventre on his mother's. He was born in 1940 in Browning, a town of two thousand in northwest Montana that serves as the headquarters and trade center for the Blackfeet Reservation. He attended schools on the Blackfeet and Fort Belknap reservations, ultimately graduating from high school in Minneapolis. He attended Minnesota University and Northern Montana College, and received a B.A. from the University of Montana. He went on to teach in the creative-writing program there for two years before leaving teaching to devote more time to writing.

Welch published his first collection of poems, *Riding the Earthboy Forty,* in 1971.[1] Earthboy was the name of a family from Welch's reservation; the "forty" refers to the number of acres in their allotment of land. The poems are drawn from Welch's Montana experiences.

Although some of Welch's poetry is perfectly clear, even to an unsophisticated reader, much of it is difficult to understand. Like many other recent American poets—James Dickey, Kenneth Koch, John Ashbery, Robert Bly, and James Wright, to name just a few—he has been influenced by surrealism.[2] His poems are most directly influenced by the poetry of his friend James Wright, who died in 1980, and the works of the Peruvian poet Cesar Vallejo.

Surrealism has its roots in earlier European movements like dada and symbolism, but as a self-conscious movement it began with André Breton's 1924 publication of *Manifeste du Surrealisme.* The object of the surrealists was to free art from the logical, realistic way of viewing and depicting things. Surrealists wanted to create a new order of reality, a new way of seeing, which merged dreams with waking perceptions, the real with the imaginary, the conscious with the unconscious. Association of unlike ideas and the linking of seemingly disparate objects in striking images became the distinguishing mark of their poems.

Breton had been a student of psychiatry before World War I and as an intern practiced psychotherapy with the wounded during the war. After the war, when his interest changed from medicine to poetry, he retained his interest in Freud's ideas. He and the other surrealists attempted to draw on the unconscious as a source of art, primarily through the methods of automatic writing, self-induced mental aberrations, and dreams.

The surrealists recorded and analyzed their dreams, and some of them, most notably Robert Desnos, were able to dream and then recall the images they had dreamed. These images were an important element in their poetry and paintings.

Breton and Paul Éluard experimented extensively with the simulation of abnormal mental states. They imitated delirium and other forms of insanity with the hope of inducing their minds to apprehend the connections and associations between objects which would serve as the basis of their art.

Automatic writing was, in effect, a form of self-administered psychoanalysis. Anna Balakian writes that by "placing themselves in a state of stupefying attentiveness they tried to shut out all outside disturbances and to give free association to words and the images which these suggested."[3] The *Textes Surrealistes* of Éluard and Tristan Tzara are examples of automatic writing which are remarkable for their bizarre and striking imagery.

If the use of the unconscious was one major innovative thrust of the surrealists, the other was their radical change in use of language. Language was important not for its ideas (the surrealists believed that poetry should not convey ideas or describe emotions) but for its images—images that exist independent of a subject, and make no logical sense. Examine, for instance, these images from Benjamin Peret's poem "Quatre à Quatre":

And the stars that frighten the red fish
are neither for sale nor for rent
for to tell the truth they are not really stars but apricot pies
that have left the bakery
and wander like a traveler who missed his train at midnight
in a deserted city whose streetlamps groan because of
their shattered shades.[4]

or this one, from André Breton's "Tiki": "I love you on the surface of the seas / Red like the egg when it is green."[5] Surrealists were also interested in the way certain sounds of words suggested certain meanings. These examples from Michael Leiris's *Glossaire* are typical: "revolution—solution de tout reve" (revolution—dream solution); "humain—la main humide" (human—the damp hand).[6]

There is often a lighthearted absurdity in the writing of the first generation of surrealists, Breton and his confreres. In the Spanish and South American surrealists who followed them there is a grimmer use of the same techniques. Robert Bly has said that "One distinction between Spanish surrealism and French surrealism is that the Spanish 'surrealist' or 'leaping' poet often enters into his poem with a heavy body of feeling piled up behind him as if behind a dam. As you begin the Spanish poem, a heavy river rolls over you."[7]

In place of the lighthearted absurdity of Peret's apricot pies, we are given images like this one from Frederico Garcia Lorca's "Little Infinite Poem":

I saw two mournful wheat heads made of wax
burying a countryside of volcanoes;
and I saw two insane little boys who wept as they leaned on a
murderer's eyeballs.[8]

The South American who influenced Welch the most
was Cesar Vallejo, a Peruvian poet (1892-1938). Except for
a brief exile in Spain, when the French deported him for his
Marxist activities, Vallejo spent most of his adult life in Paris.
Vallejo was a *cholo*—a man of mixed white and Indian
origin—and he incorporates his ethnic heritage into his poetry. Translator John Knoepfle says that

> there is something very ancient in this Vallejo which gives
> his voice a force a reader seldom confronts. It is the authority
> of the oral poets of the Andes, those fashioners of the "harawi,"
> a mystical, inward-turning complaint. Its tones can still be
> heard in lyrics sung in the mountains of Peru and played
> on the records in the homesick barrios of Lima. Born in the
> Andes of an Indian mother, Cesar Vallejo took this folk form
> in its essentials, discarding what was superficial and pic-
> turesque, and made it the echo chamber for a modern and
> surrealistic speech.[9]

Vallejo had published two volumes of highly imagina-
tive, symbolic poems before Breton's *Manifeste* appeared,
and he found surrealistic techniques congenial. In the thirties
surrealist poets came to the position that dreams were not
poetry, and so rather than recording their dreams they wrote
dreamlike poems, poems that reproduced the atmosphere or
ambiance of dreams but were composed by the same creative
processes as traditional poetry. In these poems, as in dreams,
objects undergo strange transformations, and normal, everyday causality is suspended, but the works are carefully disci-
plined products of the conscious imagination.

It is difficult in a limited space to convey much about
Vallejo's poetry, but these few fragments may give at least
some impression of the nature of his work:

> I know there is someone
> looking for me day and night inside her hand,
> and coming upon me, each moment in her shoes.

Doesn't she know the night is buried
with spurs behind the kitchen?[10]

And what if after so much history, we succumb,
not to eternity,
but to these simple things, like being
at home, or starting to brood!
What if we discover later
all of a sudden, that we are living
to judge by the height of the stars
off a comb and off stains of a handkerchief!
It would be better, really,
if it were all swallowed up, right now![11]

There is in Vallejo a deep pessimism and scene of absurdity. He couples a passionate intensity toward life with
a fatalism that human effort is wasted, human life is hopeless. Although he often writes about God, he is basically an
existentialist: God is not dead, but he is in very poor health.
"Well," he writes, "on the day I was born, God was sick."[12]
God, like man, finds the universe a burden: "Spring returns;
it returns and will go away. And God curved in time repeats
himself, and passes, passes with the backbone of the universe on his shoulder."[13]

Welch came to Vallejo through James Wright. He read
Vallejo chiefly in the translations done by Wright, Robert
Bly, and John Knoepfle. To say that Wright and Bly discovered Vallejo for American poets is probably an overstate-
ment, but they did a great deal through their edition of his
poems, and through Bly's magazine *The Seventies,* to bring
him to the attention of the community of American Poets.

Wright was born in 1927 in Martin's Ferry, Ohio, a coal-
mining town across the river from Wheeling, West Virginia.
Like Vallejo, he is from a working-class family:

My father toiled fifty years
At Hazel-Atlas Glass,

71

Caught among the girders that smash the kneecaps
of dumb Honyaks.[14]

Although Wright became a college professor and so, unlike
Vallejo, was able to escape poverty, he retained an empathy
for the outcasts—winos, whores, bums—and wrote of them
often and sympathetically. Wright also wrote happy poems
of open fields (for example, "A Blessing," "Trying to Pray,"
"Today I was Happy, so I made this Poem," all from *The
Branch Will Not Break*), but the dominant tone of his poetry
is one of bleakness, and his works are full of the images
of the coal mines—slag piles, ponds of creosote, and the
"open graves of stripmines."[15]

Like Vallejo's, Wright's poems express a defeated existentialism. God is not dead, or even sick, but he is extremely
remote, unfeeling, and unconcerned with man. "And my
bodies—father and child and unskilled criminal— / Ridicu-
lously kneel to bare my scars, / My sneaking crimes, to
God's unpitying stars."[16]

The most striking religious figure in Wright's works is
Judas. In "St. Judas" the fallen disciple tells of how, when
he has gone out to commit suicide, he saves a man from being
beaten by hoodlums, and "Flayed without hope, / I held the
man for nothing in my arms."[17] Judas is the hopeless sinner
and loser who appears in other guises in Wright's poems—
drunk, murderer, prostitute—whose act of kindness is un-
dertaken not out of hope of reward, for that is gone, but
simply out of the goodness of his heart—"for nothing." God
is not dead as far as these losers are concerned, but he has
ceased caring about them.

Wright's surrealism is a sometimes thing. Many of his
poems are straightforward and realistic, with a surrealistic
image here and there; others resemble the dreamlike works
of Vallejo:

I am frightened by the sorrow
Of escaping animals.

72

The snake moves slowly
Beyond his horizon of yellow stone.
A great harvest of convicts has shaken loose
And hurries across the wall of your eyes.[18]

Women are dancing around a fire
By a pond of creosote and waste water from the river
In the dank fog of Ohio.
They are dead.[19]

In tone Wright's poems resemble those of the Spanish surrealists more than the French. The passionate feeling, the bitter cynicism, the weary feeling of defeat, and the sense of anomie in an absurd universe that occur in the poetry of Lorca, Vallejo, and Pablo Neruda is what comes through in Wright's verse.

Welch shares the existentialism and surrealism of Vallejo and Wright. Welch's existentialism is largely the result of the disillusionments of reservation life and a tribal and personal habit of laughing at the absurdity of existence. Welch acknowledges his interest in Vallejo and Wright, and as their outlook was congenial to his, he borrows their surrealistic techniques.

"Magic Fox" is a good example of what I mean by Welch's surrealism:

They shook the green leaves down,
those men that rattled
in their sleep. Truth became
a nightmare to their fox.
He turned their horses into fish,
or was it horses strung
like fish, or fish like fish
hung naked in the wind?

Stars fell upon their catch.
A girl, not yet twenty-four
but blonde as morning birds, began
a dance that drew the men in

73

green around her skirts.
In dust her magic jangled memories
of dawn, till fox and grief
turned nightmare in their sleep.

And this: fish not fish but stars
that fell into their dreams.[20]

Explicating surrealist poems is always a dubious business, and so I hesitate to say very much about "Magic Fox." T. S. Eliot once said that "genuine poetry can communicate before it is understood,"[21] and so the poem may transmit something to readers even if they can not say what it is about. However, there is no doubt that it is better to understand intellectually as well as intuitively what Welch is doing in "Magic Fox."

"Magic Fox" is about dreaming: it is a dreamlike description of dreamers. The rules governing the poem are those of the world of dreams. The dreamers, "those men that rattled in their sleep," dream of leaves, horses, fish, stars, and a beautiful girl. The dreams are controlled by a magic fox, a sort of trickster figure, a being with power to transform things (not unlike a poet, in fact). The fox transforms the dreamers' horses into fish—or does he?—the dreamers are not sure, because the world of dreams is always uncertain, and images shift constantly.

The surrealist poem speaks through its images, and these must be apprehended by intuition rather than ratiocination. For instance, a girl "as blonde as morning birds" makes no logical sense but perfect poetic sense to anyone who appreciates blondes and songbirds. The image evokes the girl's freshness, her outdoorsy, sunstriken, dewy beauty. The girl draws the "men in green around her skirts." Welch is not using green in any denotative sense, but the term makes sense poetically in that green is the color of blooming nature, and fits with the image of morning birds. The men swirling green around her skirts remind the reader of the green leaves in the first line. There is a connection between the leaves, men, fish, and stars that fall and swirl throughout the poem. Although Welch is not recording a dream the way the first surrealists did, his poem of an imagined dream imitates the process of dreaming. His description is hazy, indefinite, a pastiche of fragments, full of familiar yet strange occurrences and transformations. In short, what Welch is doing is depicting a dream in language that is as vivid, indefinite, and troubling as dreams often are.

In the first edition of *Riding the Earthboy Forty*, "Magic Fox" was well back in the book, the first poem of the third section, "Knives." The first poem of the book was "Day after Chasing Porcupines," a straightforward, nonsurrealistic description of a scene from a Montana reservation farm. In the newest edition, published in 1976, Welch has changed the order of the poems, moving "Knives" to the front, and "Magic Fox" is now the first poem in the book. Most of the poems in "Knives" are surrealistic, and by placing them where they are the first poems the reader encounters, Welch has indicated that surrealism has become the dominant mode of his poetic voice and vision.

Dreaming is a motif that runs through many of Welch's surrealist poems. "Dreaming Winter," also from the "Knives" section, reads in part:

> Wobble me back to a tiger's dream,
> a dream of knives and bones too common
> to be exposed. . . .
>
> Have mercy on me, Lord. Really. If I should die
> before I wake, take me to that place I just heard
> banging in my ears. Don't ask me. Let me join
> the other kings, the ones who trade their knives
> for a sack of keys. Let me open any door,
> stand winter still and drown in a common dream.[22]

75

Meaning is elusive in a poem of this sort, but it appears that Welch is contrasting the old Plains Indian way of life, hunting and warfare, with the uncertain world that the Indian now inhabits. The tiger is a predator who symbolically stands for the Indian as hunter and fighter, and the dream of knives is the memory of the old life. But that life is over, for better or worse, and so the hunter must trade his knife for the keys to the real world. Welch's attitude toward this new world is ambiguous. The "Really" in the last stanza indicates that the prayer may be more ironic than fervent. Whatever the tone, the door Welch mentions leads to life in the white world, and drowning in a common dream means participating dubiously in American mainstream culture. "Winter" refers not only to that fierce season that ravages Montana but also to the winter in the blood that is the subject of his novel.

In "Picnic Weather" dreams seem to represent the unconscious, and art is the defense the subject of the poem erects against the frightening images that emerge from the unconscious mind.

> I know the songs we sang,
> the old routine, the dozen masks
> you painted when we left you
> alone, afraid, frightened of yourself
> the day the bull snakes rose,
> seething out of dreams, has made you
> what you are—alone, afraid, stronger.
>
> Here we go again. The same sad tune.
> You knew you would die some night,
> alone, no folks, and I, no face, alone,
> weaker in the knees and in the heart.
> Picture this as your epitaph:
> the bull snakes rising against you,
> you popping their necks with a clean jerk
> and the sky the drab blue of spring.
>
> Winter now: here your image dies.

I can't grab hold of you like the snakes.
I know the dream: you, alone, stronger
than the night I popped your neck,
left you squirming on the ground, afraid
you'd find your hole and disappear,
and me, my fingers strong around your head,
my head making clicking sounds—
nothing like the music in your bones.[23]

The snakes that rise seething from dreams seem to sym-
bolize dark, frightening sexual threats from within the mind
itself. The songs that the subject of the poem sings and the
masks he paints seem to represent the subject's art as a
defensive response to these frightening urges. But in "Picnic
Weather," as in "Magic Fox," the images shift and change
as in a dream. In the second stanza the subject pops the
neck of the snakes; in the third stanza the subject becomes
a snake himself, and the poet pops his neck.

Although surrealism is French in origin, and comes to
Welch from South America by way of a white American
poet, there is an Indian connection—a reason why surrealism would be a congenial mode of expression to a Blackfeet
poet—and that is the importance of visions to Plains Indian
culture.

The vision quest was a widespread phenomenon among
many American Indians but figured most importantly in the
culture of the plains tribes. A youth approaching manhood
would go to a remote place on the prairie and, with fasting
and often self-torture, would await a vision that would serve
as the basis of the youth's spiritual life from that time forward.

Among the Blackfeet it was more common for mature
men than for young boys to attempt the quest. Many failed
in their attempt to have the vision. The Blackfeet warrior
was to abstain from food or drink for four days and nights
and he was obliged to seek a place that involved some

77

danger, either from terrain or predatory animals. The vision, if it came, usually arrived in the form of some animal that gave the seeker power and advised him of the course his life should take.[24]

There is an obvious relation in the way that both the surrealist and the Blackfeet perceive visions and dreams as experiences outside and above—that is, more important than—waking reality, which give meaning to everyday life. In fact, the surrealists were aware of this connection, and in the thirties they studied Indian cultures in North and South America whose rituals included the vision quest.

Welch is familiar with Blackfeet vision traditions, as he reveals in "Getting Things Straight":

> Is the sun the same drab gold?
> The hawk—is he still rising, circling,
> falling above the field? And the rolling day,
> it will never stop? It means nothing?
> Will it end the way history ended when
> the last giant climbed Heart Butte, had his vision,
> came back to town and drank himself
> sick? The hawk has spotted a mouse.
> Wheeling, falling, stumbling to a stop,
> he watches the snake ribbon quickly
> under a rock. What does it mean?
> He flashes his wings to the sun, bobs
> twice and lifts, screaming
> off the ground. Does it mean this to him:
> the mouse, a snake, the dozen angry days
> still rolling since his last good feed?
> Who offers him a friendly meal?
> Am I strangling in his grip?
> Is he my vision?[25]

The poem is an existential statement about Welch's search for meaning in his life. He wonders whether the hawk he sees might be his vision. That the poem ends

78

with a question rather than an answer indicates that he has not found a meaning, that the hawk has nothing to tell him. The allusion to the giant's vision quest indicates why.

The giant who undertook his vision quest on Heart Butte symbolizes the last Indian who was able to find meaning in the old culture. He was a giant during his quest, but much reduced in stature when he returned to the white bar in town and drank himself sick. In the Montana that Welch depicts in his novel and poems, Indians drift in and out of white towns and bars, estranged from their traditional culture and the security and meaning it afforded them. Welch is saying that history ended for the Indians when their traditional way of life ended, and days that were once filled with meaning for them are now meaningless. History is over, and the gods are dead; events continue to transpire, but there is no pattern to existence, only dreams of the past.

Welch's poems obviously lack the playful humor of French surrealist verse, but a close look reveals a bitter humor and caustic wit. Perhaps this humor should not surprise us; Welch's novel, *Winter in the Blood,* is a comic novel. But the tone of Welch's poems is less genial than that of the novel; the humor is more fierce—and the laughter it calls forth is of a very uneasy sort. Welch uses humor as a weapon against white bigots in poems like "My First Hard Springtime" and "Harlem Montana: Just off the Reservation," but he also directs it against Indians because much of the time he seems to find people ludicrous, and he believes that the only honest response is satire. Welch objects to the sentimentally romanticized portraits of Indians by white poets:

I have seen poems about Indians written by whites and they are either sentimental or outraged over the condition of the

79

Indian. There are exceptions . . . but for the most part only an Indian knows who he is . . . and hopefully he will have the toughness and fairness to present his material in a way that is not manufactured by conventional stance.[26]

In essence, Welch's view of life is existential, and although his perspective is not as absurdist as that of Beckett or Ionesco, his heroes, like theirs, are antiheroes, floundering about in a meaningless universe. There is something of the fool or clown in many of Welch's characters, not only those in *Winter in the Blood* like Lame Bull, the Airplane Man, or even the protagonist, but also the figures in the poems: Earthboy, Bear Child, Speakthunder, Grandma's Man, and, most importantly, the persona of the poet himself in "Arizona Highways," "Plea to Those Who Matter," and "Never Give a Bum an Even Break."

Acquaintance with Blackfeet religion may shed light on why Welch so often depicts people as fools. Napi, or Old Man, the chief deity and culture hero of the Blackfeet, is also often depicted as a fool. Like most Indian culture heroes Napi is a trickster, a complex figure who is alternately creator and destroyer, savior and menace, prankster and buffoon.

In the stories in which Napi acts as creator, he is depicted in reverential terms. In the tales like those in which the coyote tricks him and eats his dinner, or in which he is chased and almost killed by a big rock he has offended, Napi is depicted as an irresponsible fool. He is a footloose figure of enormous appetites, whose hunger almost results in the extinction of rabbits and whose sexual exploits were notorious (these stories, unfortunately, were rarely translated into English, probably because of the prudery of most early American anthropologists).

Every Blackfeet Welch's age no doubt grew up with a steady diet of Napi stories, and the shape of the peripatetic god who is both a fool and a philanderer lurks in the background of much of Welch's work, like the figures in his poems and the hero of *Winter in the Blood*.

In considering Welch's portrayal of himself, let us consider "Arizona Highways," a poem in which he explores his reaction to a young Navajo girl he has met while touring Arizona giving poetry readings:

I see her seventeen,
a lady dark, turquoise
on her wrists. The land
astounded by a sweeping rain
becomes her skin. Clouds
begin to mend my broken eyes.

I see her singing by a broken shack,
eyes so black it must be dawn.
I hum along, act sober,
tell her I could love her
if she dressed better, if her father
got a job and beat her more.
Eulynda. There's a name
I could live with. I could
thrash away the nuns, tell them
I adopt this girl, dark,
seventeen, silver on her fingers,
in the name of the father, son,
and me, the holy ghost.
Why not? Mormons do less
with less. Didn't her ancestors
live in cliffs, no plumbing,
just a lot of love and corn?
Me, that's corn, pollen
in her hair. East, south, west, north—
now I see my role—religious.
The Indian politician made her laugh.
Her silver jingled in her throat,
those songs, her fingers busy
on his sleeve. Fathers, forgive me.
She knows me in her Tchindii dream,
always a little pale, too much
bourbon in my nose, my shoes
too clean, belly soft as hers.

81

I'll move on. My schedule
says Many Farms tomorrow, then
on to Window Rock, and finally home,
that weathered nude, distant
as the cloud I came in on.[27]

The title of the poem is an ironic reference to the slick magazine of the same name—a sort of Chamber of Commerce publication encouraging tourists to visit the colorful Grand Canyon state. Welch's sardonic outlook is the antithesis of the perpetually upbeat magazine's.

Before discussing Welch's relationship to the girl, it is necessary to make the point that when a poet depicts himself in a work, the "I" is a persona, a character or an artistic creation, not a realistic self-portrait. There is, of course, a resemblance between poet and persona, and the poet is the basis of the characterization, but the persona that appears in the poem should not be confused with the poet himself. The picture of Welch in "Arizona Highways"—the pale, flabby poet with a noseful of bourbon—is an exaggeratedly comic portrayal of the man who wrote the poem, much as Chaucer, the "elvyssh popet" who tells the doggerel tale of Sir Thopas, is a caricature of the author of *The Canterbury Tales.*

The setting of "Arizona Highways" is a bar. Eulynda is talking to an Indian politician. She is dark-skinned, with black eyes. She is poorly dressed but wears turquoise bracelets and silver rings. She seems thoroughly at home not only in the bar but also in her cultural milieu. Moreover, the imagery of the poem links her to the land: "The land / astounded by a sweeping rain / becomes her skin."

In one sense this means that her skin is red brown like the earth, but in a deeper sense it means that the girl is still a part of the Indian culture that has its roots in the earth, and so to Welch she is of the earth, earthy, in a way that he no longer is. Of course it must be realized that Indian culture in the 1970s consists as much of Levis, Coors, and jukeboxes as it does of hogans and horses, and Eulynda is no more Indian genetically or by virtue of her upbringing than Welch, a full-blood who was born and raised on a reservation. But Eulynda is Indian culturally because she lives the way most Arizona Indians live now, and Welch has been cut off from his ethnic identity by his college education and his profession of poet.

Welch feels out of place in the Indian bar, an unfit companion for Eulynda. He feels white ("a little pale"), flabby ("belly soft as hers"), and overdressed ("my shoes too clean"). In short, he feels that he is too civilized—not pure enough for a woman like Eulynda. Since he would not do as her lover, he ironically suggests alternative relationships: a paternal (he would adopt her) or spiritual one (he would be Holy Ghost to her Virgin Mary, or medicine man putting pollen in her hair). But there is something very wrong between them. He is like a Tchindii to her. Tchindii are Navajo ghosts, the spirits of the dead, a malevolent and vengeful pack who often bedevil the living. Welch is afraid that he seems alien, frightening, wraithlike, insubstantial, malevolent to Eulynda.

In short, the persona that Welch depicts is a caricature— pale, pudgy, spectral, and overdressed. He realized that there is no relationship that he can establish with Eulynda and so decides to move on down the highway.

Without making too much of it, it is perhaps worth mentioning the resemblance between Welch's "lady dark" and the Dark Lady of Shakespeare's sonnets. Shakespeare actually consummates his relationship with his paramour and is filled with self-loathing, while Welch, who leaves the bar without even speaking to Eulynda, feels much the same way about himself. The similarity lies in the ambivalent attitudes—passion mixed with disdain—of the pale poets about their dark, earthy women.

In "Plea to Those Who Matter," Welch's persona becomes that of a clown. Here Welch examines the question

83

of ethnic identity from a very different standpoint. Whereas in "Arizona Highways" Welch was not Indian enough, here he is too Indian.

You don't know I pretend my dumb.
My songs often wise, my bells could chase
the snow across these whistle-black plains.
Celebrate. The days are grim. Call your winds
to blast these bundled streets and patronize
my past of poverty and 4-day feasts.

Don't ignore me. I'll build my face a different
    way,
a way to make you know that I am no longer
proud, my name not strong enough to stand
    alone.
If I lie and say you took me for a friend,
patched together in my thin bones,
will you help me be cunning and noisy as the
    wind?

I have plans to burn my drum, move out
and civilize this hair. See my nose? I smash it
straight for you. These teeth? I scrub my teeth
away with stones. I know you help me now I
    matter.
And I—I come to you, head down, bleeding from
    my smile,
happy for the snow clean hands of you, my
    friends.[28]

The poem is difficult to understand until Welch explains the situation behind it. Welch's wife-to-be, a non-Indian English teacher in the University of Montana, was invited to a department party; Welch, who at that time was also in the department, was not invited. In the poem Welch expresses his belief that his Indianness has caused his exclusion. He feels his Indian past of "poverty and 4-day feasts" makes him inferior in the eyes of the white professors, and he pleads for a chance to change himself—to burn his drum, the symbol of Indianness, to civilize his unruly hair and straighten his nose, so that he will be welcomed by their snow-white hands.

The poem, like "Arizona Highways," is about identity, which, it appears, is a matter of context: who you are depends on where you are and who you are with. A man is a child to his parents and a parent to his children. A professor may be a pedant to his students but a good old boy to his teammates on a gas-station softball team. Welch sees himself as a paleface to Eulynda but as a savage to the University of Montana English Department.

The experience is obviously painful, and Welch treats it with a mordant irony. The tone is darker than that of "Arizona Highway"; Welch again plays the buffoon in mock self-abasement, but the hyperbolic fantasies he depicts ("I scrub my teeth away with stones") are savage in their intensity. This clown is battered—nose smashed, "bleeding from his smile." Although the pose is one of self-abasement, the poem is an attack on his fellow professors, the comedy a weapon.

This clownish persona appears again in the last poem of *Riding the Earthboy Forty*, "Never Give a Bum an Even Break." Welch speaks of leaving home with a friend and then concludes: "Any day we will crawl out to settle / old scores or create new roles, our masks / glittering in a comic rain." *Persona* is, of course, the Latin word for *mask*. Here Welch's persona speaks of donning a mask to face the comic (that is, absurd) world, or, simultaneously, of donning a comic mask as a way of coping with the world.

Welch applies the same acerbic irony to others as well as himself. "Grandma's Man" is about a wise fool, a man who neglects his farm in order to paint.

> That day she threw the goose over the roof
> of the cowshed, put her hand to her lips
> and sucked, cursing, the world ended. In blood

85

her world ended though these past twenty years
have healed the bite and that silly goose
is preening in her favorite pillow.

Her husband was a fool. He laughed too long
at lies told by girls whose easy virtue disappeared
when he passed stumble-bum down the Sunday
    street.
Baled hay in his every forty, cows on his alloted
    range,
his quick sorrel quarter-horse, all neglected for
the palms of his friends. Then, he began to paint
LIFE.

His first attempt was all about a goose that bit
the hand that fed it. The obstacles were great.
Insurmountable. His fingers were too thick to
    grip
the brush right. The sky was always green
the hay spoiled in the fields. In wind, the rain,
the superlative night, images came,
    geese
skimming to the reservoir. This old man listened.
He got a bigger brush and once painted the cry
of a goose so long, it floated off the canvas
into thin air. Things got better. Sky turned white.
Winter came and he became quite expert at
    snowflakes.
But he was growing wise, Lord, his hair white as
    snow.

Funny, he used to say, how mountains are blue
in winter and green in spring. He never ever
got things quite right. He thought a lot about
    the day
the goose bit Grandma's hand. LIFE seldom came
the shade he wanted. Well, and yes, he died well,
but you should have seen how well his friends
    took it.[29]

The painter is known to us only as "Grandma's Man": in the eyes of the narrator of the poem he is not even man enough to be called "Grandpa," much less to be called by his given name. The narrator relates the first stanzas of the poem from Grandma's point of view, and so our introduction to Grandma's Man is as Grandma's husband, the fool. Before he started painting, Grandma's Man neglected his farm to drink in town with his friends. He was a figure of fun, too much of a stumble-bum even for the women of easy virtue he lurched past on Sunday mornings. The narrator refers snidely to his "allotted range," the implication being that Grandma's Man is an Indian who has received his land as a dole from the government. When he begins to paint, he remains a fool in the eyes of his wife and friends, but the narrator implies that he thereby gains a certain wisdom, and that he becomes superior to the people who ridicule him.

Grandma's Man finds his vocation suddenly, apocalyptically, as it were: "The day she threw the goose over the roof of the cowshed . . . the world ended." It ended not only for the goose, who is dispatched for having bitten the hand that fed it; it ends also for Grandma and her man, for the incident provides the inspiration for his first picture (like Welch, Grandma's Man has a fondness for subjects that combine pain and comedy). Unfortunately, he is not much of a painter, partly because of his simpleminded approach to painting. He wants to paint LIFE. The capital letters stress the banality of Grandma's Man's conception.

Nonetheless, although beset with physical and conceptual difficulties, Grandma's Man perseveres until he achieves a measure of proficiency—"he became quite expert at snowflakes." More important, his painting makes him more aware of the world than he has ever been before. Painters, even bad painters, look more closely at familiar things than do other people, and consequently see much more than non-painters. To the average person a tree is a green mass; to a painter it is many different colors and combinations of light and shade. Grandma's Man's observation that mountains are blue in winter and green in spring may not seem startling, but he is one of the few people in his valley who looks at the mountains at all.

Like many artists, Welch concerns himself with the question of the artist as a misfit in society. But he avoids a cliché treatment of the subject here by making the artist a mediocre painter. It is not that some yokels are scoffing at a rural Picasso. Their critical faculties may be undeveloped, but by and large Grandma's Man's critics are right about the quality of his work. Nonetheless, the sensitivity Grandma's Man has developed from the discipline of painting has elevated him above the critics who deride him.

Welch's irony in these lines is marvelous: "He laughed too long / at lies told by girls whose easy virtue disappeared / when he passed stumble-bum down the Sunday / street" and "Well, and yes, he died well, / but you should have seen how well his friends / took it."

Grandma's Man never becomes a good painter—"LIFE seldom came the shade he wanted"—but that is not important. He is a drinker and dreamer, a fool in the eyes of his wife and friends, but his art has given him a far greater wisdom and humanity than the people who laugh at him possess. In this respect he is a wise fool in the tradition of Don Quixote—a man who tilts at windmills but is more human than the wiser citizens around him.

"In My Lifetime" is another poem about a wise fool, but unlike "Grandma's Man" it contains very little humor:

This day the children of Speakthunder
run the wrong man, a saint unable
to love a weasel way, able only to smile
and drink the wind that makes the others go.
Trees are ancient in his breath.
His bleeding feet tell a story of run
the sacred way, chase the antelope naked

till it drops, the odor of run
quiet in his blood. He watches cactus
jump against the moon. Moon is speaking
woman to the ancient fire. Always woman.

His sins were numerous, this wrong man.
Buttes were good to listen from. With thunder-
hands his father shaped the dust, circled
fire, tumbled up the wind to make a fool.
Now the fool is dead. His bones go back
so scarred in time, the buttes are young to look
for signs that say a man could love his fate,
that winter in the blood is one sad thing.

His sins—I don't explain. Desperate in my songs,
I run these women hills, translate wind
to mean a kind of life, the children of Speakthunder
are never wrong and I am rhythm to strong medicine.[30]

Speakthunder is not only a fool but a wrong man, that is,
a man whom the white world at least considers wrong. He
is an ambiguous figure, simultaneously a saint and a sinner,
a demigod and a man, a hero and a fool.

He is saintly by virtue of his adherence to ancient religious rituals like the antelope hunt, and because he is incap-
able of deviousness ("unable to love a weasel way").

But he is also a sinner, a philanderer. In this he is
like his spiritual father, the Blackfeet god Thunder, a powerful deity with a dual nature. According to Blackfeet myth,
Thunder is benevolent in that he brings the rain that makes
the vegetation grow, but malicious in that he steals men's
wives.[31] Although Speakthunder is a man, he also seems to
be more than human, in that Thunder shapes him directly
from dust, fire, and wind. But, although he is a demigod
and hero, he is also a fool, a man who can only smile as
others pass him by.

Now Speakthunder is dead, and his children, tradition-
alist Blackfeet, "run the wrong man," that is, they keep his
memory alive by celebrating the rituals he loved. Welch runs

too. Composing his verse, the product and sign of his desperation, he ranges over the breast-shaped hills in the belief that the children of Speakthunder are in tune with life and that he can attune himself to their strong medicine.

James Welch is a poet with a comic way of viewing the world and a fondness for surrealism. Strange as it may appear to white readers, both of these traits can be traced to his Blackfeet heritage. The Blackfeet, who at times take a comic view of their chief god, certainly see the foolish side of men as well. With the importance of the vision to Blackfeet culture, it is not surprising that a Blackfeet poet responds to the surrealists' fascination with the world of dreams.

Chapter 6

WINTER IN THE BLOOD

Welch and the Comic Novel

WELCH'S NOVEL, *Winter in the Blood,* is a masterpiece of comic fiction. It is the narration of a nameless protagonist, a man in his early thirties, a Blackfeet, like Welch, who drifts back and forth from his mother's farm on the reservation to the bars in Havre. The narrator becomes afflicted with emotional frostbite, winter in his blood, after the death of his brother Mose, who is run over and killed by an automobile when the narrator is twelve, and by that of his father shortly thereafter, who, walking home drunk from a night in town, loses consciousness and dies of exposure. The narrator's mother Teresa marries a man named Lame Bull, a genial, somewhat clownish adventurer who wants Teresa for her prosperous farm. The hero resents Lame Bull but prefers living with him and Teresa to getting out on his own.

Much of the action of the book centers around the narrator's search for Agnes, a Cree girl whom he falsely tells his mother he has married. He lives with Agnes a short while and then disappears, leaving her with his hostile family, who despise her (the Crees were traditional enemies of the Blackfeet). Soon she returns to the bars and beer joints of Havre, and the narrator searches for her there.

There is little resolution in the book. Although the narrator finds Agnes, she will not come back with him, and her brother beats him up. But later, in a moment that bears resemblance to a Joycean epiphany, the hero discovers the identity of his grandfather and the unhappy history of his grandmother. The book does not end with this discovery, however; nor does the information appear to have much impact on the narrator's subsequent behavior.

This summary does not sound very funny, and, as with *House Made of Dawn,* readers look for and so find in *Winter in the Blood* a protest, the bitter lament of an angry writer.[1] Welch is capable of anger in poems like "Harlem, Montana: Just off the Reservation," and "In My First Hard Spring-time,"[2] but he has many other moods as well, and *Winter in the Blood*, although powerfully moving in places, is primarily comic.

Once one abandons the idea that all Indian novelists must be angry, it is not surprising to find that *Winter in the Blood* has a strong comic undercurrent. The comic novel is becoming the dominant genre in fiction today. Ishmael Reed, Thomas Pynchon, John Barth, Donald Barthelme, Kurt Vonnegut, Joseph Heller, Phillip Roth, and Stanley Elkin differ widely from one another, but their vision of the world is fundamentally comic. And Welch, although he is geographically isolated in Montana, is well aware of literary trends. As we have seen, much of his poetry is influenced by the surrealism that Robert Bly and James Wright imported from South America, and in his fiction Welch employs his own variation of the black humor used by Reed, Pynchon, and others.

Before discussing *Winter in the Blood* as a comic novel, perhaps I had better define the term. Traditionally, genres have been more sharply defined in drama than in fiction. Donatus and Evanthius, fourth-century grammarians whose commentaries on the comic dramatist Terence were appended to his work, were extremely influential in determining Renaissance ideas of comedy. These ideas, put into practice by such playwrights as Shakespeare and Jonson, determined the shape of comedy for centuries. Essentially Donatus and Evanthius defined comedy on the basis of characterization (modest estate of the characters, or "mediocrity of human fortune," Evanthius called it),[3] of tone (light, or "pleasingly witty," in Evanthius's phrase),[4] and of denouement—the fact that it has a happy ending, one usually involving the marriage of the hero and the heroine (incorporation into society and its institutions being an age-old

93

hallmark of comedic form, just as exile is an identifying characteristic of tragedy).

These distinctions are less helpful in differentiating types of novels. We can no longer identify novels on the basis of their ending, for instance. Although Jane Austen's novels end happily with marriage, many comic novels today end with the thwarting or discomfiture of the hero. In others, the hero is in no better shape than when we found him at the outset. Nabokov's Pnin has lost his job as well as his wife. Roth's Portnoy is no closer to maturity or stability than he ever was. Heller's Yossarian is literally as well as figuratively at sea. What is more, noncomic novels—for example, *A Portrait of the Artist, House Made of Dawn,* and *Ceremony*—often end on a positive note.

Methods of characterization give us some basis for differentiation between comic and noncomic[5] novels, but only if we discard the notion of status, whether in the sense of rank as the Romans and Greeks conceived it, or in the sense that Northrop Frye uses it to describe the hero of the high- and low-mimetic modes.[6] Not only is rank or status irrelevant as an indication of seriousness in contemporary fiction, but it was also irrelevant to Shakespeare, who used a duke as the protagonist in *Twelfth Night.* And, as Frye points out, although the low-mimetic mode, the one in which the hero is "one of us," is the mode of most comedy, it is also the mode of much realistic fiction.[7] Furthermore, the ironic mode—in which the hero is inferior in power or intelligence to ourselves—can be used not only for farcical comedy but also for works like *The Scarlet Letter* and *Billy Budd,* in which Hester Prynne and Billy Budd are *pharmakoi,* or scapegoats.

If the author endows his character with a sufficient dignity, if he displays compassion toward him or her—whether it is a high-mimetic hero like Hamlet or an ironic one like Billy Budd—the character has a tragic or at least serious dimension. If the author undercuts the character's dignity,

94

holds him up to ridicule either by description or by placing him in a ridiculous situation, the result is comedy. There is pathos in the situation of Humbert Humbert, Yossarian, Portnoy, and Welch's narrator, but all are treated comically. It is tone, however, that is the primary basis of the general understanding of what makes a novel comic. By and large, a comic novel is a longish work of fiction that contains a liberal amount of humor—or to put it most concisely, a funny book. On the basis of this definition, *Winter in the Blood* qualifies as a comic novel. The first sentence of the book should let us know what sort of novel we will find: "In the tall weeds of the borrow pit, I took a leak and watched the sorrel mare, her colt beside her, walk through burnt grass to the shady side of the log and mud cabin."[8] There is no lofty seriousness here, just a man performing a function that everyone, whatever he might protest to the contrary, finds funny and undignified. Scatology, which plays an important part in the novel, as we shall see at the climax of the book, has always been an important ingredient of comedy. Chaucer, Rabelais, and Faulkner use scatology as a way of making people absurd and comical.

Welch's humor varies from raucous farce to subtle satire, and it informs every corner of the novel. The broadest humor is in scenes like the one in which the unknown man dies face down in his oatmeal, or the one in which the hero and the airplane man march through the streets of Havre, the hero carrying a teddy bear and the airplane man carrying five boxes of chocolate-covered cherries under his arm. Most of the humor is verbal, however. Welch makes masterful use of ironic diction to undercut the dignity of his characters. Here for example, is Lame Bull:

> Lame Bull had married 360 acres of hay land, all irrigated, leveled, some of the best land in the valley, as well as a 2000-acre grazing lease. [P. 13]

We brought in the first crop, Lame Bull mowing alfalfa,

snakes, bluejoint, baby rabbits, tangles of barbed wire, sometimes changing sickles four times in a single day. [P. 23]

Lame Bull's hand was in a sling made from a plaid shirt.
The more he drank the more the sling pulled his neck down,
until he was talking to the floor. The more he talked to the
floor the more he nodded. It was as though the floor were
talking back to him, grave words that kept him nodding
gravely. [P. 31]

Welch's general technique, which he uses most skillfully
in the final scene of the novel, the grandmother's funeral,
is to begin a description as though he were investing a
character with some dignity, and then to pull the rug out
from under him suddenly:

I had to admit that Lame Bull looked pretty good. The but-
tons on his shiny green suit looked like they were made of
wood. Although his crotch hung a little low, the pants were
the latest style. Teresa had shortened the legs that morning,
a makeshift job, having only had time to tack the original
cuffs up inside the pants legs. His fancy boots with the
walking heels peeked out from beneath the new cuffs. . . .
Teresa wore a black coat, black high heels, and a black
cupcake hat. . . . Once again she was big and handsome—
except for her legs. They appeared to be a little skinny, but
it must have been the dress. [Pp. 173-74]

However many funny things we find in *Winter in the
Blood,* two questions arise: How much humor is enough to
make a novel comic, and what happens if in addition to the
humor there is a good deal of pathos?

It is impossible to give a quantitative answer to the first
question, but both questions can be answered at once if we
say that in most key situations of a comic novel the author
plays it for laughs rather than for pathos. Hamlet has some
funny lines, and so does Mercutio, but in their climactic
scenes *Hamlet* and *Romeo and Juliet* are tragic. There is
some genuine pathos in *Winter in the Blood,* the most

obvious example being the death of Mose. But in the most important scenes—the epiphany in which the hero recognizes his roots, and the ending—Welch deliberately opts for comedy.

Let us begin with the epiphany, to use Joyce's term, the sudden revelation of truth which is supposed to transform the hero's way of looking at the world. The truth that the hero discovers is that Yellow Calf, the man who saved his grandmother from dying of starvation and exposure, is his grandfather. The deaths of the narrator's father and brother have left him with winter in his blood—he is numbed, unable to feel love or compassion for anyone. He feels no closeness toward his mother—"Teresa never gave much" is the way he sums her up—and very little toward Agnes, the girl he abandons while he goes on a bender for several days. At the beginning of the book he describes his reluctant homecoming: "Coming home to a mother and an old lady who was my grandmother. And the girl who was thought to be my wife. But she really didn't count. For that matter none of them counted; not one meant anything to me" (p. 2).

The "old lady who was my grandmother" becomes more real to the narrator when Yellow Calf, the man he discovers to be his grandfather, tells him the story of how Blackfeet cast her out to die during one terrible winter. The narrator sees her as a young, beautiful, and vulnerable woman, whereas before he had thought of her as bloodless and superannuated. In a flash of insight he realizes that Yellow Calf is the hunter who had provided her with meat and kept her alive: that discovery moves the narrator first to laughter, then to tears. It is a special kind of laughter that has nothing to do with humor: "It was the laughter of one who understands a moment in his life, of one who has been let in on the secret through luck and circumstance. . . . And the wave behind my eyes broke" (p. 158). Reynolds Price, in reviewing the book, describes the "beautifully surprising narrative means" that Welch uses in the scene, and goes on to say of it: "Welch's new version of the central scene in all narrative literature (the finding of lost kin) can stand proudly with its most moving predecessors in epic, drama, and fiction."⁹ Perhaps so, but Price is missing a point here; there is a key difference between this scene and the reunion of Odysseus and Telemachus, for instance, and that difference is the element of farce that Welch uses in introducing the epiphany:

> I thought for a moment.
> Bird [his horse] farted.
> And it came to me, as though it were riding one moment of the gusting wind, as though Bird had had it in him all the time and had passed it to me in that one instant of corruption. [P. 158]

Welch uses scatology to undercut the sentimentality of the moment.

Perhaps the funniest and most successful scene in the novel is the ending. Normally funerals are not the stuff of comedy, since death is not something people usually laugh about. But anything, if properly treated, can be a source of humor, and Welch succeeds in making the funeral comic.

House Made of Dawn also ends with the death of a grandparent of the hero, and so some interesting comparisons present themselves. In both books the grandparents who die have served as links binding the hero to his past and to his traditional culture. When Abel's grandfather dies, Abel buries him in the prescribed Tanoan manner, and then goes out to run in the race for good hunting and harvests that his grandfather had once won. This episode marks the first time since his return from the army that Abel has been able to participate meaningfully in a Tanoan ritual, and it marks his reentry into his native culture. In an important sense it is for Abel a happy ending, although it is certainly not comic.

Since Welch's narrator has just learned the story of his

grandmother's life and has been moved by it, we might expect Welch to treat the old lady's death and burial with seriousness, showing how the narrator has developed closer ties to his culture, or at least showing that he has a new respect and deeper feeling for his grandmother. This is not the case: the narrator feels only ironic detachment toward his grandmother. After describing what Lame Bull and Teresa are wearing, the narrator says, "The old lady wore a shiny orange coffin" (p. 174). Moreover, Lame Bull and the narrator fail to make the grave large enough for the coffin, and Lame Bull must climb into the pit and jump up and down on the box containing the mortal remains of his mother-in-law in order to get her buried.

Lame Bull's eulogy for the old woman is a masterpiece of left-handed praise: "here lies a simple woman . . . who devoted her life to . . . rocking. . . . Not the best mother in the world . . . but a good mother notwithstanding . . . who could take it and dish it out . . . who never gave anybody any crap" (pp. 176-77). As counterpoints to Lame Bull's speech there are the random thoughts of the hero, who is not sufficiently interested in the proceedings to keep his mind on them. He thinks that the weather would probably be good for fishing, that maybe he ought to see a doctor about his leg, and that maybe if he got a few drinks into Agnes and proposed to her he could win her back. Obviously Welch's hero is not gripped by emotion in this scene, and Welch is not treating the funeral as a tragic occasion.

Winter in the Blood ends, as it began, on a comic note. In between, the tone varies from pathos (the scene in which Mose is hit by a car) to farce (the scenes in the hotel bar with the airplane man). But throughout most of the book, and certainly in the key scenes, the tone is richly comic.

Much literature, whether narrative or dramatic, consists of a small number of vividly depicted scenes, which serve as climaxes, surrounded by a good deal of buildup and filler. These scenes, tableaux of a sort, often sum up a major theme of the work, and seem to be a quintessence of the whole. For instance, there is the scene at the end of *1 Henry IV*, after the Battle of Shrewsbury, when Hal stands between the prostrate bodies of Hotspur, who has died for honor, and Falstaff, who is feigning death because he has no honor. In a sense Hal is a mean between these extremes. Another such tableau is the scene in which Moby Dick pulls Ahab out of the whale boat while the Pequod sinks, bringing down the sky-hawk folded in Ahab's flag. A visual summation of *The Scarlet Letter* occurs when Hester, Pearl, and Dimmesdale stand on the platform while a scarlet "A" blazes in the sky, and Chillingsworth watches from below.

There are two such scenes in *Winter in the Blood*, one climactic and one anticlimactic, joined by the narrator's memory and visual motifs. The first is the death of Mose, presented in a flashback as the narrator remembers the incident. One important element of the scene is that the narrator stresses that it is a distant memory, the recollection of an event that was not clear at the time:

> It was dusk, that time of the day the light plays tricks on you, when you think you can see better than you actually can, or see things that aren't there. The time of day your eyes, ears, nose become confused, all become one gray blur in the brain, so you step outside your body and watch the movie of a scene you have seen before. [P. 140]

In the climactic, tragic scene, the narrator and Mose have rounded up the family's cattle and driven them from the range to the gate of their land. One recalcitrant cow, a "wild-eyed spinster" who has been leading the herd, balks at going through the gate. As she stands there, a calf breaks, and Bird, the narrator's horse, instinctively gives chase. The narrator is too small to control the horse and can only cling to the saddle horn. As this is happening a car flies past, hitting his brother's horse and killing Mose. Although the narrator could not have seen the accident, he has a distinct picture of it in his mind:

> I couldn't have seen it—we were still moving in the oppo-site direction, the tears, the dark and wind in my eyes—the movie exploded whitely in my brain, and I saw the futile lurch of the car as the brake lights popped, the horse's shoulder caving before the fender, the horse spinning so that its rear end smashed into the door, the smaller figure flying slowly over the top of the car to land with the hush of a stuffed doll. [P. 142]

This is one climax of the book; this accident is the ultimate source of the narrator's problems. He falls from Bird, injuring his leg. He loses his brother, and because of his brother's death his father drinks more, eventually killing himself. His father and brother are the only people the narrator has ever loved, and so after the accident he goes through life crippled emotionally as well as physically.

The penultimate scene of the book, in which the narrator unsuccessfully tries to save another cow, echoes the scene we have been discussing. The elements are the same: a cow causing problems, a horse out of control, and a narrator who watches helplessly as death occurs. The horse is still Bird, who is very old by now, and, although the cow in trouble is not the same as the spinster, it has the same wild look in its eye and seems to be a sort of bovine doppelgänger: "I had seen her before, the image of catastrophe, the same hateful eye, the long curving horns, the wild-eyed spinster leading the cows down the hill into the valley" (p. 166). The cow has gotten stuck in the slough and is drowning in the mud as if it were quicksand. The narrator manages with difficulty to get a rope over its head and, with Bird pulling, they get the cow partly out of the slough before Bird loses his footing and falls. The cow drowns and Bird dies, apparently from the overexertion of his rescue effort.

The scenes are paired opposites: one tragic, one comic; one climactic, one anticlimactic. The first is a tragic moment in the comic book: death strikes the narrator's brother. In the second, the cow dies, and Bird dies, but neither is a serious loss to the narrator. In fact, to minimize the effect of the loss and to keep the reader from feeling much sympathy for the animals, or the narrator for losing them, Welch mentions the deaths very obliquely: "The cow down in the slough had stopped gurgling" (p. 172), and "The red horse down in the corral whinnied. He probably missed old Bird" (p. 176). The scenes are linked by the narrator's sense of déjà vu and by their common elements, which are, in fact, the quintessential elements of the Western—cow, cowhorse, and cowboy. But the mode of *Winter in the Blood* is not heroic and romantic, like that of the horse opera, but ironic: the cowboy is an Indian, and the horse is out of control.

Because the reference to the cow's death is oblique, readers like Michael Dorris argue that the narrator has saved the cow and that this small triumph indicates larger ones to come,[10] somewhat like the scene in *Shane* in which the farmers pull out the stump (the comparison is mine, not Dorris's). According to Dorris the narrator's success, coupled with his thoughts at the funeral about proposing to Agnes, indicate that his winter in the blood is breaking up, and that spring in the blood cannot be far behind.

But a careful reading shows that the cow is dead, and that furthermore the narrator does not care: "Some people, I thought, will never know how pleasant it is to be distant in a clean rain, the driving rain of a summer storm. It's not like you'd expect, nothing like you'd expect" (p. 172). Nothing has changed. The narrator tries to save the cow, but as usual he cannot seem to win for losing. He is at peace with himself for the moment, but if we read what he thinks to himself about Agnes at the funeral ("Next time I'd do it right. Buy her a couple of crèmes de menthe, maybe offer to marry her on the spot" [p. 175]), it is obvious—

because of the need for drinks, and the "maybe"—that his resolution to "do it right" is idle daydreaming. Winter lasts a long time in Welch's Montana.

Leslie Marmon Silko

Chapter 7

LESLIE SILKO'S *CEREMONY*

A LAGUNA GRAIL STORY

LESLIE SILKO is of Laguna, Mexican, and white ancestry. Born in 1948 in Albuquerque, she grew up at Laguna, in west-central New Mexico. Despite her keen awareness of the equivocal position of mixed-bloods in Laguna society, she considers herself Laguna. As she puts it: "I am of mixed-breed ancestry, but what I know is Laguna."[1]

The Lagunas are a Keresan Pueblo people, whose culture is similar to that of the Jemez Momaday writes about in *House Made of Dawn* and *The Names*. Laguna Pueblo is a cosmopolitan place where some Hopi, Zuni, Navajo, Zia, Santa Ana, Jemez, Cochiti, Domingo, and Acoma live with the Laguna.[2] Despite this melange, the Laguna have a keen idea of their discrete identity, and Silko's sensitivity to being of mixed ancestry is painfully apparent in her depiction of Tayo in the novel *Ceremony*.

Silko's great-grandfather was a white surveyor and trader named Robert Gunn Marmon, who came to Laguna in 1872, four years after his brother Walter had moved there. The brothers settled in the pueblo, and both eventually served as governor.[3] Although the pueblo governor traditionally did not have as much power and prestige as the chief religious leader, he was nonetheless an important man in community affairs.

Being a Marmon Laguna, a mixed-blood from a ruling family, meant being different from, and not fully accepted by, either the full bloods or the whites. This was a source of pain to Silko, but it was also a source of creative sensitivity. As she puts it:

My family are the Marmons at Old Laguna on the Laguna Pueblo reservation where I grew up. We are mixed bloods—

106

Laguna, Mexican, white—but the way we live is like Marmons, and if you are from Laguna Pueblo you will understand what I mean. All those languages, all those ways of living are combined, and we live somewhere on the fringes of all three. But I don't apologize for this any more—not to whites, not to full bloods—our origin is unlike any other. My poetry, my storytelling rise out of this source.[4]

Silko attended the University of New Mexico, graduating with a B.A. in English in 1969. She stayed on at the university and taught creative writing and a course in the oral tradition for the English department. Silko has published a collection of poems, *Laguna Woman,* and some short stories,[5] but by far her best work is her novel, *Ceremony.*

Ceremony is the story of a mixed-blood Laguna named Tayo who, lacerated by the desertion of his mother, the contempt of the aunt who reared him, and the trauma he experienced as a soldier in World War II, has severe mental problems. White doctors are unable to cure him, but, by the efforts of a Navajo medicine man named Betonie and a mysterious woman named Ts'eh Montano, with whom he has a love affair, Tayo achieves a complete recovery.

During the time of Tayo's illness the Laguna reservation is suffering from an extreme drought. When Tayo recovers, the land blooms again. Silko intersperses Laguna myths throughout the narrative. These myths give Tayo's story an added dimension—a timelessness, or a sense that the action has happened before and will happen again. Because of this dimension, Momaday calls *Ceremony* a "telling" rather than a novel: "Leslie Silko's *Ceremony* is an extraordinary novel, if indeed 'novel' is the right word. It is more precisely a telling, the celebration of a tradition and form that are older and more nearly universal than the novel as such."[6] Momaday is referring to Indian narratives, of course, but *Ceremony* also belongs to another tradition and form older than the novel—the grail romance.

Critics have long recognized that twentieth-century novelists like Hemingway, Fitzgerald, and Malamud employ features of the legend of the Holy Grail in their fiction.

107

It is important to note, however, how these authors use the legend. In *The Sun Also Rises* and *The Great Gatsby*, Hemingway and Fitzgerald consciously use the wasteland of the grail legend to provide a central symbol for their works and to give both the action and the characters a suggestion of universality. In *The Natural*, a comic novel, Malamud incorporates the grail legend as part of the parody, and, although the tone of his novel is quite different from that of *The Sun Also Rises* and *The Great Gatsby*, the grail legend functions symbolically in much the same way to universalize the story.

Leslie Silko's *Ceremony* is a very different kind of book. Silko was not familiar with the grail legend at the time she wrote *Ceremony*,[7] but because Laguna mythology and beliefs are similar in a number of important ways to medieval European beliefs, Silko's novel is similar to the grail legend. Both are based on the fundamental idea that a man's health and behavior have grave consequences for his land.

Many versions of the story of the grail appear in medieval romance, but essentially the legend tells about a maimed Fisher King who has been gravely wounded in the groin. As the king languishes, his land suffers as well; it is afflicted by a severe drought and becomes a wasteland. In the Fisher King's castle there is a mysterious Holy Grail, the cup used by Jesus at the Last Supper. A knight—Gawain, Percival, or Galahad—comes to the castle in search of the grail, and cures the king while he is there. When the king recovers, his land blooms. Not all the versions contain the same details, but this is a composite of the story in its different forms.[8]

Twentieth-century versions of the grail legend, from Eliot's to Malamud's, ignore the grail and concentrate on the wasteland. Eliot's *The Wasteland* has had an enormous influence on the literature of this century, prose as well as poetry, and is probably the most important piece of grail literature since Malory. Eliot was strongly influenced by Jesse Weston's *From Ritual to Romance,* a work of anthropological criticism that interprets the grail story as a Christianized version of ancient vegetation cults.

Eliot makes the drought-stricken wasteland and the maimed Fisher King the central symbols of his poem. Although his later works were strongly Christian, the dominant tone of *The Wasteland* is of existential despair over the sterility and "terrible dreariness of great modern cities."[9] There is no grail in Eliot's poem. Unlike the medieval legends, it ends not with the recovery of the Fisher King and his land but with the king's death and continued drought.

Fitzgerald and Hemingway were influenced by Eliot rather than by any medieval version of the myth, and they too focus on the wasteland rather than the grail. Although Fitzgerald makes fleeting mention of a quest for a grail, it is one that ends tragically for the quester.[10] Gatsby is the quester, and Daisy is the grail he pursues, but there is a profound irony in Fitzgerald's implied analogy between the sacred cup of medieval legend and the empty-headed and callous (if charming) heroine of *The Great Gatsby*. To Fitzgerald it is Gatsby's quest, not the object he seeks, that is admirable—a profound shift from the medieval emphasis. Fitzgerald depicts the East as a moral wasteland, but his most striking use of the wasteland as a symbol is his description of the Valley of Ashes in Queens, where George Wilson, though hardly a king, has been metaphorically wounded in the groin by Tom Buchanan's horning. The novel would not be much changed if there was no mention of the grail legend, but, as it stands, the legend adds a faint wash of symbolic coloration to the story.

The same could be said of Hemingway's treatment of the legend in *The Sun Also Rises*. Jake Barnes, the hero, a fisherman by avocation, has been wounded in the groin during World War I and as a result is impotent. The setting of the book, the Europe of the expatriate, is a spiritual wasteland peopled by a lost generation of wanderers. Although Jake undergoes a great deal of mental suffering, there is no grail or knight to guide him, and he is not cured at the end of the novel. The title of the book, taken from Ecclesiastes, suggests that the earth will endure and spring will follow winter, but there appears to be no hope of recovery for Hemingway's hero. Hemingway uses the myth to suggest that his characters are acting in roles played many times before in the universal drama—that, as Ecclesiastes puts it, there is nothing new under the sun.

Malamud's *The Natural* is a marvelously funny novel about a baseball player with a magic bat. Malamud weaves a great deal of baseball lore into his story, a comic version of the grail legend. Pop Fisher (who is wounded in his hands, not his groin) is the manager of the New York Knights, a team whose woeful fortunes are reflected in the drought that has afflicted their city. Roy Hobbs, the hero, whose exploits with his magic bat resemble those of Gawain with his lance, leads his team almost to the pennant. He fails, however, and ends in disgrace. Malamud is doing comically what Hemingway and Fitzgerald do more seriously, using the grail legend to provide a symbolic dimension to the action of the book.

In contrast to these novels, which merely use the grail legend to provide a symbolic backdrop, *Ceremony* is an Indian analog of the grail legend. The heart of the grail legend in its early versions is the link between a man's health and the fate of his land. In *From Ritual to Romance,* her classical study of the grail legends, Jessie Weston concludes:

> To sum up the result of the analysis, I hold that we have solid grounds for the belief that the story postulates a close connection between the vitality of a certain King and the prosperity of his kingdom; the forces of the ruler being weakened or destroyed, the land becomes Waste, and the task of the hero is that of restoration.[11]

The chief similarity between *Ceremony* and the grail leg-ends—and it is a fundamental one—is that there is a link between Tayo's condition and the drought that has laid waste his land. Tayo plays the role of the wounded king, Betonie is the healer, and the Laguna reservation is the wasteland.

The ultimate cause of Tayo's illness is a centuries-old "witchery," and Betonie's ceremonial cure is completed by Tayo's sacred quest. Tayo's illness and the drought in New Mexico is traced to Tayo's behavior during World War II. During the war Tayo and his cousin Rocky are stationed on a nameless Pacific island fighting the Japanese. When Rocky is wounded, Tayo and another soldier carry him on a litter through the drenching rain. Tayo fears the effect of the rain; it is bothering Rocky's wound and turning the road to mud so that the soldier carrying the other end of the litter keeps slipping. Tayo prays for the rain to stop:

> When Tayo prayed on the long muddy road to the prison camp, it was for dry air, dry as a hundred years squeezed out of yellow sand, air to dry out the oozing wounds of Rocky's leg, to let the torn flesh and broken bones breathe, to clear the sweat that filled Rocky's eyes. . . . He wanted the words to make a cloudless blue sky, pale with a summer sun pressing across wide and empty horizons. The words gathered within him and gave him strength. . . . he could hear his own voice praying against the rain. [Pp. 11-12]

What directly follows this scene in the text is the Laguna myth of Reed Woman, who spends all her time bathing while her sister Corn Woman works in the sun. When Corn Woman scolds Reed Woman for bathing, Reed Woman goes away to

> the original place
> down below.
>
> And there was no more rain then.
> Everything dried up

111

                    all the plants
                     the corn
                     the beans
                  they all dried up
                and started blowing away
                     in the wind.

               The people and the animals
                     were thirsty.
               They were starving. [Pp. 13-14]

It is not clear whether this is a part of Tayo's prayer or simply an interpolation of myth, but the result of the prayer is obvious. Following the myth, the narrative picks up the story in New Mexico after the war: "So he had prayed the rain away, and for the sixth year it was dry; the grass turned yellow and it did not grow. Wherever he looked Tayo could see the consequences of his praying" (p. 14). Tayo's guilt about Rocky's death and the drought causes him a nervous breakdown:

> For a long time he had been white smoke. He did not realize that until he left the hospital, because white smoke had no consciousness of itself. It faded into the white world of their bed sheets and walls; it was sucked away by the words of doctors who tried to talk to the invisible scattered smoke. He had seen outlines of gray steel tables, outlines of the food they pushed into his mouth, which was only an outline too, like all the outlines he saw. They saw his outline but they did not realize it was hollow inside. He walked down floors that smelled of old wax and disinfectant, watching the outlines of his feet; as he walked, the days and seasons disappeared into a twilight at the corner of his eyes, a twilight he could catch only with a sudden motion, jerking his head to one side for a glimpse of green leaves pressed against the bars on the window. He inhabited a gray winter fog on a distant elk mountain where hunters are lost indefinitely and their own bones mark the boundaries. [Pp. 14-15]

Tayo is suffering from what, in medical terms, is probably catatonic schizophrenia. Silko is not writing from the point of view of white medicine, although she might well be familiar with the symptomatology. It is important here to keep in mind the distinction between the author and what Wayne Booth calls the "implied author," that is, the literary creation whose views are the views of the work.[12] Leslie Silko is a college professor, well aware of modern psychiatric medicine, but Leslie Silko, the author of *Ceremony,* is writing from the viewpoint of a traditional Indian. If Silko were having a breakdown, I would guess that she would be more likely to visit a psychiatrist than a medicine man like Betonie, but that has nothing to do with this novel. Given the values of the "implied" Leslie Silko, Tayo can be cured only by Indian medicine.

The views of the implied author often differ sharply from those of the actual author. For instance, Christopher Marlowe was an outspoken atheist, and yet *Dr. Faustus* is a profoundly Christian work. The author of a ghost story need not believe in ghosts, but the implied author must. Likewise, there is an implied reader who suspends his normal beliefs. Most Americans do not believe in demonic possession, but, when reading *The Exorcist* (or seeing the film), virtually everyone thinks that the mother is wasting her time taking her possessed daughter to the psychiatrist; Catholics and non-Catholics, believers and cynics, want the mother to get the girl to a priest as soon as possible. And whatever white— or Indian—readers think of medicine men, we want Tayo to go to one instead of to a psychiatrist. I point this out at length to help the reader avoid a simplistic, reductive reading of *Ceremony.* Many of those whites who characterize them-selves as "being on the Indians' side" want Indians to reject white society completely in favor of some form of pristine cultural purity. To some extent skepticism toward white American society may give Indians pride in their heritage, but to what extent is it really possible or even desirable in twentieth-century America to return to nineteenth-century living patterns? Silko can teach at a state university, drive a car to work, eat spaghetti, and take aspirin for headaches without compromising her integrity. In *Ceremony,* however, Tayo must find his cure and salvation within an Indian context. His cure must come from a medicine man rather than from a white doctor. The medicine man uses some paraphernalia from white civilization, but, however eclectic his medicine bundle, his cure is fundamentally Indian. There is integrity in this too. But it is also important to remember that *Ceremony* is a fiction—a literary creation that Silko consciously composed while sitting in her house (in Alaska, as it happened); it is not a mystical vision she received while sitting in a kiva in a holy trance. The values in *Ceremony* are Indian, and the message is that Indians are best off when they remain within their traditional culture (even though that is constantly changing) and that the old gods still have power. The book was written, however, by a woman who is white as well as Indian, and whose profession is writing poems and novels and teaching in a predominantly white university.

Given the values of the "implied" Leslie Silko, Tayo must be cured by a medicine man. The man, Betonie, is an old mixed-blood Navajo. There is an irony in having a Navajo cure a Laguna, because the Navajo and Laguna tribes were traditional enemies. In the eighteenth century, in fact, the Laguna made an alliance with the Spanish to protect themselves from Navajo raids.[13] The raids continued until late in the nineteenth century, and the animosity lasted long afterward, although Silko makes no mention of it.

Betonie is part Mexican, like Silko, and that they are both mixed-bloods is a bond between him and Tayo. In accord with his mixed origins, Betonie's curative techniques are highly eclectic. The description of his hogan is interesting in this regard:

114

Tayo sat down, but he didn't take his eyes off the cardboard boxes that filled the big room; the sides of some boxes were broken down, sagging over with old clothing and rags spilling out; others were jammed with the antennas of dry roots and reddish willow twigs tied in neat bundles with old cotton strings. The boxes were stacked crookedly, some stacks leaning into others, with only their opposing angles holding them steady. Inside the boxes without lids, the erect brown string handles of shopping bags poked out; piled to the tops of the Woolworth bags were bouquets of dried sage and the brown leaves of mountain tobacco wrapped in swaths of silvery unspun wool.

He could see bundles of newspapers, their edges curled stiff and brown, barricading piles of telephone books with the years scattered among cities—St. Louis, Seattle, New York, Oakland—and he began to feel another dimension to the old man's room. [Pp. 119-20]

Betonie explains to Tayo that a modern medicine man needs and uses the artifacts of white American civilization. At first Tayo thinks the old calendars and phone books are just junk, but later he realizes that Indians live largely in the white world today, and Indian medicine encompasses things from the white world that touch Indians.

The particular cure that Betonie gives Tayo is the bear cure. Silko appends the story, which Betonie tells as part of his cure, about how Coyote bewitched a man and how the man's mother-in-law and grandfather took him to the summit of Dark Mountain to see the four old Bear People who had "the power to restore the mind." The Bear People cured the bewitched man by preparing four hoops, four bundles of weeds, and a white-corn sand painting. Betonie then takes Tayo to the summit of a mountain, from which no traces of civilization can be seen, and, seating him in the center of a white-corn sand painting, treats him with the bundles and hoops, while Betonie's helper imitates a bear.

Betonie makes it clear that the ultimate cause of Tayo's

illness, and the real enemy, is "the witchery." Witches in Southwest Indian culture are very similar to those of medieval Europe; they are human beings who oppose the divine sources of good and devote themselves to the worship and performance of evil through their sorcery. In medieval Europe witchcraft was not a separate religion from Christianity, the way Buddhism is; it was rather a mirror image of Christianity. Christians worshiped God and hated the Devil; witches worshiped the Devil and hated God. The chief Christian ceremony was the mass; for witches it was the black mass— the mass recited backwards. Witches said the Lord's Prayer backwards and hung crosses upside down.

Indian witches despise the gods that pious Navajos and Pueblos worship. Witches worship evil gods instead, and devote themselves to harming the religious and god-fearing. According to Betonie their most devastating weapon is the white man, whom they have invented for the purpose of causing harm to their fellow Indians. Betonie tells Tayo that he must realize that the whites are not the real enemy; it is the witchery. Betonie alerts Tayo to the true nature of the enemy and helps him participate in the religious ritual of the bear cure. Tayo completes his cure by completing his sacred quest—finding his Uncle Josiah's cattle and bringing them home.

Josiah had bought a special kind of hardy Mexican cattle that he thought might survive in the harsh desert of New Mexico. The cattle are footloose and attempt to return to Mexico, moving south every time they can get through reservation fences. After Josiah dies, the cattle become lost. Betonie tells Tayo that he sees in Tayo's future an alignment of stars, a mountain, and a woman. Tayo sets out and arrives at the house of a woman named Ts'eh Montano, who lives at the foot of a mountain, on the evening that the stars appear. Ts'eh tells Tayo that she knew he was coming, and they become lovers. With her help he is able to bring the cattle home.

Ts'eh Montano is in some ways like Silko herself—a young, attractive, restless, mixed-blood Laguna woman—and it is hard to believe that in some ways Ts'eh is not a self-portrait. But Ts'eh is also a good deal more; she appears to have psychic powers, and there is even a hint that she is a sacred figure of some sort:

> It took a long time to tell them [the tribal elders] the story; they stopped him frequently with questions about the location and the time of day; they asked about the direction she had come from and the color of her eyes. . . .

A'moo'ooh, you say you have seen her
Last winter
up north
with Mountain Lion
the hunter

All summer
she was south
near Acu

They started crying
the old men started crying
"A'moo'ooh! A'moo'ooh!
You have seen her
We will be blessed
again. [P. 257]

There is some link between Ts'eh and the she-elk that Ts'eh shows Tayo, because the priests cry "A'moo'ooh! A'moo'ooh!" at that, too, but the link is ambiguous. Silko leaves it ambiguous deliberately. When asked about it, she said that she knows her characters as "acquaintances that she visits," and so she does not know everything about them.[14]

Making love to Ts'eh has a therapeutic effect on Tayo (p. 181), as does his absorption in the hunt for the cattle (p. 129). When he is able to recapture the cattle, the accomplishment of that task and his love for Ts'eh restore him to

117

health. At that point his land blooms again:

> The valley was green, from the yellow sandstone mesas in the northwest to the black lava hills in the south. But it was not the green color of the jungles, suffocating and strangling the earth. The new growth covered the earth lightly, each blade of grass, each leaf and stem with space between as if planted by a thin summer wind. There were no dusty red winds spinning across the flats this year. [P. 219]

What remains is for Tayo to defeat Emo, the chief of the villains, the witchery's agents. On one level it appears that Emo is more victim than villain—an Indian veteran used by a racist government to defend a way of life he cannot really participate in. But on a more profound level Emo is a villain whose links with supernatural evil give him power to manipulate even the whites.

> "One thing," she said finally, looking down at the red coals in the ring of white ash, "there are only a few others with Emo. The rest have been fooled; they're being used. Tools. The Army people don't know. They don't know about stories or the struggle for the ending to the story. White people are always busy. They will ask themselves: what is one Indian veteran living in a cave in the middle of some reservation? They won't have much time for you. The only reason they come is because Emo called them." [P. 232]

It is clear that the burden of the struggle falls on Tayo, and that much more than his personal health or happiness is at stake: "Old Betonie shook his head. 'This has been going on for a long long time now. It's up to you. Don't let them stop you. Don't let them finish off this world'" (p. 152). This is not the absurd, inflated claim of a deluded medicine man. Here Betonie clearly speaks for the implied author.

Curiously, Tayo's method of fighting is passive. He sits and watches while Emo and Pinkie torture Harley. He is sorely tempted to try to kill Emo:

It had been a close call. The witchery had almost ended the story according to its plan; Tayo had almost jammed the screwdriver into Emo's skull the way the witchery had wanted, savoring the yielding bone and membrane as the steel ruptured the brain. Their deadly ritual for the autumn solstice would have been completed by him. He would have been another victim. [P. 253]

But Tayo restrains himself. As a result, Harley and Pinkie die, and Emo is banished from New Mexico, while Tayo lives in triumph.

The happy ending of the novel is a surprise to most readers, because they expect the customary tragic ending of a protest novel with the Indian protagonist as victim—something like the tragic end of the fictionalized Ira Hayes of *The Outsider,* dead of drink in a ditch.

But this is not a protest novel; it is a form that blends myth with realistic fiction, and the myth calls for a happy ending. Silko juxtaposes the happy ending of Tayo's story, and the story of his land, with the happy ending of the myths that she has interlarded all along. After watching Pinkie and Emo drive off with Harley's body, Tayo thinks:

He would go back there now, where she had shown him the plant. He would gather the seeds for her and plant them with great care in places near sandy hills. The rainwater would seep down gently and the delicate membranes would not be crushed or broken before the emergence of tiny fingers, roots, and leaves pressing out in all directions. The plants would grow there like the story, strong and translucent as the stars. [P. 254]

"The transition was completed" Silko says; Tayo has gone from sickness to health, and the reservation from drought to verdure. Silko adds this myth:

Hummingbird and Fly thanked him.
They took the tobacco to old Buzzard.

119

"Here it is. We finally got it but it
sure wasn't very easy."
"Okay," Buzzard said
"Go back and tell them
I'll purify the town."
And he did — [P. 255]

Tayo is the buzzard that purifies his town. The last myth
of the book says of the witchery

It is dead for now.
It is dead for now.
It is dead for now.
It is dead for now. [P. 261]

There are a number of parallels worth mentioning between *Ceremony* and the grail romances. On one level Tayo
is clearly analogous to the wounded Fisher King whose
decrepitude has afflicted his land. In performing the task of
retrieving Josiah's cattle, however, Tayo is like the questing
knight — Percival, Gawain, or Galahad — who heals the land
by his virtuous actions.

Betonie, the medicine man, is analogous to Gawain. He
is nowhere as heroic — that side of Gawain is played by
Tayo — but Gawain was a healer as well as a fighter. In
Percival, Chrétien de Troyes says, "Of wounds and healing
lore / Did Sir Gawain know more / Than any man alive."[15]
Chrétien's statement is echoed in Wolfram von Eschenbach's
Parzifal and the anonymous Dutch *Lancelot.* On the basis
of accounts of Gawain's skill, Jessie Weston speculates that
in an early stage of tradition "not only did Gawain cure the
Grail King, but he did so not by means of a question, or
by the welding of a broken sword, but by the more obvious
and natural means, the administration of a healing herb"
(p. 109) Weston goes so far as to link Gawain of the grail
legend with the doctor of popular mumming plays, a figure
who bears a close resemblance to an Indian medicine man.
As for parallels to Ts'eh, there is no shortage of women with

120

supernatural powers in the Arthurian grail romances; they vary from the hideous Cundrie of *Parzifal* to the beautiful Morgan le Fay who tempts Gawain.

There is no problem in finding correspondences between *Ceremony* and the grail legends—some close, some strained—but what is most important is the point that the two stories are based on the same myth or motif: when a man falls ill, his land becomes afflicted by drought. When he is cured, by a combination of ritual and the accomplishment of a sacred task, his land blooms again. Jessie Weston has shown that this motif has its roots in ancient fertility myths and that it exists in all corners of the globe. Silko told me that she did not know the grail romances when she wrote *Ceremony*, but she did incorporate a great body of Laguna myth into the story, and the central motif of that myth is the relationship of a man's health and behavior to the fertility of his land.

Tom Foley

Gerald Vizenor

Chapter 8

BEYOND THE NOVEL
CHIPPEWA-STYLE

Gerald Vizenor's Post-Modern Fiction

GERALD VIZENOR is a mixed-blood Chippewa or, as the Chippewas prefer to call themselves, Anishinabe.[1] His father's family was from the White Earth Reservation in northern Minnesota. Vizenor's father, Clement, who was half Anishinabe and half white, left the reservation for Minneapolis, where he worked as a painter and paperhanger for three years before he was murdered by a mugger, who nearly severed his head while cutting his throat. The chief suspect, a large black man, was apprehended but was released without being prosecuted. During the same month Clement's brother died in a mysterious fall from a railroad bridge over the Mississippi.

Gerald was twenty months old at the time of his father's murder, too young to remember him. Twenty-five years later, however, he questioned the officer in charge of investigating the crime. The detective defended his shoddy investigation by saying, "We never spent much time on winos and derelicts in those days . . . who knows, one Indian vagrant kills another."[2]

While Vizenor's mother battled poverty in Minneapolis, she sometimes kept Gerald with her and sometimes left him with his Anishinabe grandmother; sometimes she allowed him to be taken to foster families. When Vizenor was eight, his mother married a hard-drinking, taciturn mill engineer named Elmer Petesch, and this brought some stability if not joy into Vizenor's life. After eight years, however, Vizenor's mother deserted Petesch, leaving Gerald behind. After several months Vizenor also moved out, but Petesch broke his dour reserve and pleaded with Vizenor to return, and for a brief period the two lived together as

124

close friends. After five months, however, Petesch died in a fall down an elevator shaft, and Vizenor was alone again.

Given this childhood, filled with desertion and violent deaths, it is not surprising that Vizenor developed a bizarre and bloody view of the universe. Rather than reacting with despair, however, Vizenor has joined the fight against absurdity and injustice with the elan of the Anishinabe trickster Wenebojo.

Vizenor has had a varied professional career. He has served as director of the American Indian Employment and Guidance Center in Minneapolis and worked as an editorial writer for the Minneapolis *Tribune*. Currently he teaches in both the Department of Native American Studies in the University of California at Berkeley and the English Department of the University of Minnesota.

Like Momaday, Welch, and Silko, Vizenor writes both poetry and fiction. He published thirteen poems in Kenneth Rosen's *Voices of the Rainbow*,[3] for the most part mordant glimpses of Indian life in America today. He has also published a collection of haiku, the result of his experiences — as a private first-class in the army — on the Japanese island of Matsushima.

Vizenor has published a memoir of his early life entitled "I Know What You Mean, Erdupps MacChurbbs: Autobiographical Myths and Metaphors." In it Vizenor not only relates the violent and bizarre story of his childhood but also tells about his fantasy life. Erdupps MacChurbbs is one of the "benign demons and little woodland people of love" (p. 95) who people his fantasies. These little people provide a rich inner life for Vizenor and help him keep his sanity in a mad world.

> They are the little people who raise the banners of imagination on assembly lines and at cold bus stops in winter. They marched with me in the service and kept me awake with humor on duty as a military guard. The little people

125

sat with me in baronial ornamental classrooms and kept me alive and believable under the death blows of important languages.[4]

Chippewa mythology is full of stories about benign demons and little woodland people, and stories about Vizenor's Anishinabe grandmother are probably the chief source for Mac-Churbbs and his friends. However, as the name Mac-Churbbs suggests, Vizenor, like most other Americans, probably picked up some Irish fairy lore as well.

In 1978, Vizenor published a series of sketches entitled *Wordarrows: Indians and Whites in the New Fur Trade.*[5] The book is a series of sketches, principally about Anishinabe whom Vizenor met as Director of the Employment and Guidance Center. In these sketches Vizenor appears to be the Isaac Bashevis Singer of the Chippewa: he combines an extremely keen eye for detail and an appreciation for an interesting story with a scrupulous sense of honesty. The result, like that of Singer's works, is a highly revealing picture of a ghetto people—their power and dignity, flaws and foibles, and, above all, their essential humanity.

Wordarrows is an important key to understanding Vizenor's poetry. The poems, although they often deal with the same characters and subjects as the essays, are cryptic and allusive, and the reader can understand them more fully after reading Vizenor's prose pieces. For example, the nameless heroine of the poem "Raising the Flag"[6] is described more fully in the sketch "Marlene American Horse" in *Wordarrows,* and the "wounded Indian" in the poem "Indians at the Guthrie"[7] is the Rattling Hail of "Rattling Hail's Ceremonial" in *Wordarrows.*

Wordarrows also provides valuable background information for understanding *Darkness in Saint Louis Bearheart,* Vizenor's major work. The fictional framework of the book is as follows: Saint Louis Bearheart, an old man who works in the Heirship Office of the Bureau of Indian Affairs, has spent ten years at his desk in the Bureau secretly writing a manuscript entitled "Cedarfair Circus: Grave Reports from the Cultural Word Wars." When members of the American Indian Movement break into the offices of the BIA, one of them, a young Indian girl, encounters Bearheart sitting in the dark, and, after having sex with him, goes off to read the book. What she reads is what we read.

"Cedarfair Circus" is the story of a strange group of Indian pilgrims who wend their way from Minnesota to New Mexico at some future time when, because of insufficient oil supplies, American civilization has collapsed into bloody anarchy. Murderous and perverted figures hold power, among them the Evil Gambler, the fast-food fascists, and the pentarchical pensioners. The wanderers do battle with these forces of evil, sustaining heavy losses, but eventually a few of them make it to freedom.

The leader of the pilgrims is Proude Cedarfair, the last in the line of the Cedarfairs who refused to leave their ancestral home in northern Minnesota to go to the Red Cedar Reservation, the fictional name of the White Earth Reservation where Vizenor's forebears lived. Proude lives in the midst of a large circle of cedar trees named by his family the Cedar Circus (the Cedarfairs have lived as clowns and tricksters for generations, battling the evil incursions of the whites and hostile Indians with their wit).

When there is no more oil available, the government commandeers trees, and Jordan Coward, the corrupt, drunken president of the Red Cedar Reservation government, attacks the trees of the Cedar Circus. Proude decides not to confront the evil chief and the federal agents, however, and with his wife, Rosina, he sets out on his cross-country odyssey. Others join them in their wanderings, until they have assembled quite a ragtag army.

The first to join Proude and Rosina is Benito Saint Plumero, who calls himself "Bigfoot." He is a "little person, but his feet and the measure of his footsteps were twice his visual size" (p. 32). Bigfoot received his cognomen in prison while serving time for stealing from a park the bronze statue he is in love with. The Cedarfairs meet Plumero at the "scapehouse of weirds and sensitives," a survival center established (with federal funds) on the Red Cedar Reservation by thirteen "women poets" from the cities. Bigfoot has been staying at the scapehouse to provide sexual services to the weirds and sensitives with his remarkable penis, President Jackson. The most interesting of the weirds and sensitives are Sister Eternal Flame, whose "face was distorted with comical stretchmarks from her constant expressions of happiness" (p. 33); Sister Willabelle, whose body is marred by horrible scars from worms and piranhas which attacked her when her plane crashed in the Amazon jungle; and Sister Talullah, the "law school graduate [who] could not face men in a courtroom without giggling like a little girl so she concentrated on interior litigation and the ideologies of feminism and fell in love with women" (p. 39).

The Cedarfairs take Bigfoot with them and soon are joined by Zebulon Matchi Makwa, a "talking writer and drunken urban shaman" (p. 45); Belladonna Darwin-Winter Catcher, the daughter of a white reporter named Charlotte Darwin and Old John Winter Catcher, a Lakota holy man Charlotte met while she was covering the Wounded Knee episode of 1973; Scintilla Shruggles, a "new model pioneer woman" and keeper of the Charles Lindbergh house for the Minnesota Division of Historic Sites (p. 65); Iniwa Biwide, a sixteen-year-old youth who "resembles a stranger" (p. 71); Bishop Omax Parasimo, a religious master who wears a metamask with the same features as Scintilla Shruggles (p. 71); Justice Pardone Cozener, "the tribal lawyer and one of the new prairie big bellies"; Cozener's homosexual lover, Doctor Wilde Coxswain, "the arm wagging tribal historian" (p. 72); Sun Bear Sun, "the 300 pound, seven foot son of utopian tribal organizer Sun Bear" (p. 74); Little Big Mouse, "a small white woman with fresh water blue eyes" (p. 74), whom Sun Bear Sun carries in a holster at his belt; Lilith

Mae Farrier, the "horsewoman of passionless contradictions," a child-hating school teacher who is the mistress (literally) of two massive boxer dogs (p. 74); and Pio Wissakodewinini, the "parawoman mixedblood mammoth clown," a man who was sentenced to a sex change operation for committing two rapes (p. 75).

On their travels the pilgrims face and overcome a succession of enemies. First is the Evil Gambler, Sir Cecil Staples, the "monarch of unleaded gasoline," who wagers five gallons of gasoline against a bettor's life in a strange game of chance. Sir Cecil always wins, then allows losers to choose their form of death. Sir Cecil was reared on interstates by a truck-driving mother. Because Ms. Staples had been sterilized by the government (for having illegitimate children while on welfare), she took to kidnapping children from shopping malls. She stole thirteen in all, bringing them up in her truck as she drove back and forth across the country and finally turning them out at rest stops when they were grown. Staples told her children that they "should feel no guilt, ignore the expectations of others, and practice to perfection whatever [they did] in the world" (p. 122). Sir Cecil decided to practice the art of killing people.

Needing gasoline for the postal truck they have obtained, the pilgrims choose lots for who will gamble with Sir Cecil. Lilith Mae Farrier, the lady of the boxers, is selected. When she loses, Proude also gambles with Sir Cecil, with the understanding that, if he should win, Lilith lives and Sir Cecil dies. Proude wins, and kills Sir Cecil by strangling him with a "mechanical neckband death instrument," but Lilith, depressed by her loss, immolates herself and her boxers.

Back on the road, the pilgrims meet a procession of cripples: "The blind, the deaf, disfigured giants, the fingerless, earless, noseless, breastless, and legless people stumbling, shuffling and hobbling in families down the road" (p. 141). Belladonna Darwin-Winter Catcher warns the pil-

129

grims: "Never let the cripple catch your eye. These cripples are incomplete animals lusting for our whole bodies" (p. 141). Little Big Mouse ignores Belladonna's advice and performs a nude dance for the cripples, who become so excited that they pull her into hundreds of pieces.

When they reach Oklahoma, the pilgrims meet the "food fascists" who have hung three witches from the rafters of the Ponca Witch Hunt Restaurant and Fast Foods to season them before cutting them into pieces for takeout orders. The pilgrims decide to save the witches and, sneaking back at night, rescue two of them, but Zebulon Matchi Makwa, the smelly drunken urban shaman and talking writer, is overcome by desire and has intercourse with his witch in the restaurant, where they are discovered and killed by the fascists.

Belladonna Darwin-Winter Catcher is killed by a colony of "descendants of famous hunters and bucking horse breeders" (p. 185), who put to death anyone they catch espousing a "terminal creed," that is, the belief that there is only one true way. Vizenor borrows the idea of terminal creeds from Eric Hoffer's remarks about "true believers." Ridiculing terminal beliefs is a major theme in Vizenor's work, since he detests zealots, whatever their views, and particularly those who are humorless as well as narrow-minded. Belladonna's terminal beliefs, which concern the superiority of the tribal way of life, are views Vizenor finds congenial in many respects, and the people who kill her are unlovable, rigid rednecks, so the story of the death is told with a good deal of ambiguity and irony.

Many other curious events follow. Bishop Omax Parasimo is killed by lightning, and Justice Pardone Cozener and Doctor Wilde Coxswain, the homosexual lovers, decide to stay at the Bioavaricious Regional Word Hospital, a facility established by the government to investigate public damage to the language. Sister Eternal Flame catches Proude's wife Rosina and Bigfoot at fellatio and murders

Bigfoot. Proude and Iniwa Biwide travel by magic flight to Pueblo Bonito where a vision bear tells them to enter the fourth world—as bears—through a vision window in the pueblo. The novel ends with Rosina arriving at the pueblo and finding beartracks in the snow.

Clearly this is a strange book, quite different from the other Indian novels that we have discussed. We can better understand it by examining the Anishinabe and other Indian influences of Vizenor's, by taking a look at what he has written about his personal experiences, and by examining the "post-modern" novel, the tradition in which Vizenor is writing.

Tricksters and clowns are common in Indian cultures.[8] Among the Indians the trickster, under various names and guises, is usually the principal culture hero of the tribe, a figure second in importance only to the supreme god. But he is a highly ambiguous figure. As his name implies, he is primarily one who plays tricks. He is also the butt of tricks, and how often he is the tricker rather than the trickee seems to depend in part on how the tribe views itself. Some tricksters are usually successful; others are almost always the victim of tricks. Although the trickster is generally a benefactor—who in some cases creates man, brings him fire, and rescues him from enemies—he can also be a menace, because he is generally amoral and has prodigious appetites for food, sex, and adventure. He is capable of raping women, murdering men, eating children, and slaughtering animals. In fact, the trickster violates all tribal laws with impunity, to the amusement of the listeners of the tales, for whom he acts as a saturnalian surrogate.

The Chippewa trickster is called Wenebojo, Manabozho, or Nanabush, depending on how anthropologists recorded the Anishinabe word.[9] According to the myths, Nanabush is the son of a spirit named Epingishmook and Winonah, a human. His mother dies shortly after he is born, and Nanabush is reared by his grandmother Nokomis. He has

131

miraculous powers, particularly the ability to transform himself into whatever shape he wants. In his metamorphosis as a rabbit he acts as a benefactor, bringing the Chippewas fire. He saves mankind and the animals by taking them on his raft in a flood, and he teaches the Chippewa the Mide ceremonies, their most important religious rituals.

Like most tricksters, however, Nanabush is also a dangerous figure, and in one tale he murders most of his family before he realizes what he is doing.[10] In another, he marries his sister, bringing shame on himself and his family.[11]

Vizenor's conception of the trickster seems to be in line with Chippewa tradition—tricksters are benevolent but amoral, lustful, irresponsible, and given to fighting evil with trickery. Trickster tales often combine violence with humor. Tricksters are peripatetic, and trickster tales usually start, "Trickster was going along . . ." Vizenor's pilgrims, and the structure of his book, reflect this.

Sacred clowns are important in Indian religion. Although they appear to have played little part among the Chippewas, Vizenor would have heard of them from members of other tribes. Among the Sioux, Cahuilla, and Maidu, for instance, clowns performed absurd acts at the most important religious ceremonies, mocking shamans and religious leaders, pestering participants by throwing water or hot coals, dancing and cavorting, and trying to swim in shallow puddles. Among the Cheyenne, clowns acted as "contraries" who did everything backwards, saying "goodbye" when they met someone and "hello" when they left, and walking or sitting on their horses backwards. Among Pueblo tribes clowns ate feces and drank urine, pretending that they were delicious.[12]

Anthropologist Barbara Tedlock claims that the purpose of the clowns was to cause laughter, thus "opening up" spectators emotionally to spiritual forces.[13] She also argues that the mockery of sacred objects and rituals by the clowns served to show spectators that terrestrial rituals were not important. It was the meaning behind them, the higher world of the spirits, that was important.

What Tedlock says may be so, but I think that she overlooks the most important function of clowns, a function similar to the clowning at the medieval European Feast of Fools, in which once a year subdeacons sang filthy songs in church, mocked the sacrament, and threw the bishop in the river. These ceremonies allowed a saturnalian release to people whose religious and moral codes were very demanding. In a way the clowns are the reification in the tribe itself of the trickster figure of mythology; that is, they are figures who can ridicule customs, rituals, and taboos with impunity to the delight of spectators who are forced to obey them.

The Evil Gambler is a familiar figure in Indian mythology,[14] although I could not find a reference to him in the collections of Chippewa tales that I read.[15] Silko has a version of the story in the Laguna myths that she intersperses in *Ceremony*.[16] In it *Kaup'a'ta*, or the Gambler, who lives high in the Zuni Mountains, plays a stick game with people, gambling with them for their beads and clothes. By feeding his victims a combination of cornmeal and human blood the Gambler gains control over them, and they cannot stop gambling until they lose everything they own. When the victims are naked, the Gambler gives them one more play, to recoup their losses or lose their life. The Gambler has killed many victims before Sun Man, using the knowledge that his grandmother Spiderwoman gives him, is able to outwit the Gambler and kill him. Vizenor's episode of Sir Cecil Staples puts the same story into a different context.

As bizarre as *Darkness in Saint Louis Bearheart* seems, Vizenor derives much of his material from people he actually knows. Lilith Mae Farrier, for instance, the zoophilic boxer lover in *Bearheart*, was an acquaintance of Vizenor's, to whom he devotes a chapter in *Wordarrows*. Like the

133

fictional Lilith, the real Lilith was molested by her step-father on a camping trip, made a point of feeding reservation mongrels, and was thrown off the reservation by the outraged wives of the reservation officials by whom she had been propositioned. When she left the reservation, the dogs followed her van. All of them eventually dropped out in exhaustion except for two boxers that she had refused to feed (they had reminded her of her stepfather). She fed the boxers, and "In time they learned to take care of me, you know what I mean" (p. 88). The real Lilith Mae did not immolate herself, although she did have the boxers chloroformed. So, in this case, if the book is kinky, it is because the truth can be as bizarre as fiction.[17]

The combination of humor, fantasy, violence, and explicit sex that characterizes *Bearheart* is nothing new in literature: Petronius's *Satyricon*, Rabelais's *Gargantua* and *Pantagruel*, and Gascoigne's *Adventures of Master F. J.* are three of many older works one could cite that mix sex and violence with fantasy in comic fictions. But with Cervantes, and writers like Defoe and Richardson in England, the European novel turned away from fantasy, toward realism and the complexities of experience for the rising middle class. This trend reached its pinnacle with Henry James, who said, "The only reason for the existence of a novel is that it does attempt to represent life . . . the air of reality (solidity of specification) seems to me to be the supreme virtue of a novel."[18] This is not to say that nonrealistic fiction disappeared after the mid-eighteenth century, of course, but merely that it was not in the mainstream of the novelistic tradition, and often, as with science fiction, it was dismissed as subliterary.

In recent years, however, nonrealistic writers like Jorge Borges, Alain Robbe-Grillet, and Italo Calvino have emerged as major literary figures abroad, and in America in the 1970s much of the best, and even best-selling, writing has been utterly nonrealistic. Writers like Kurt Vonnegut, Richard

Brautigan, Tom Robbins, Robert Coover, Stanley Elkin, Ishmael Reed, Donald Barthelme, and Alvin Greenberg now dominate American fiction, and *Bearheart* puts Vizenor squarely in their tradition.

There has been a great deal written on the "post-modern novel" or "new fiction" as it is variously called, but in my opinion the best analysis and description is in Phillip Stevick's "Scherezade runs out of plots, goes on talking; the king puzzled, listens: an essay on the new fiction."[19] At the end of the essay Stevick proposes some "axioms" as a step toward establishing an aesthetic of the new fiction. Essentially Stevick argues that the new fiction ignores established fictional traditions to an extraordinary extent, purposely establishes a limited audience, departs from the illusionist tradition, and represents writing as play.

These things are certainly true of *Bearheart,* which is clearly a fair specimen of the post-modern novel. To expand on Stevick's points: first of all, whereas most fiction of the past centuries has reacted against some aspect of previous fiction, the new fiction simply ignores the tradition of the modern novel. Cervantes, Defoe, Fielding, Hawthorne, James, Hemingway—to name just the first novelists that come to mind—reacted against, borrowed from, parodied the writers of previous generations. Scott Momaday, the Kiowa novelist, reveals the influence of Melville, Faulkner, and Hemingway in *House Made of Dawn.* But Vizenor, like most of the post-modernists, simply ignores American writers of previous generations. He owes more of a debt to his Anishinabe grandmother than to Hemingway or Faulkner.

Second, we should note that, however much most European and American writers have railed against the philistinism of the bourgeoisie, western literature since Homer has aimed nonetheless at what Dr. Johnson called the "common reader." The new novel decidedly is not for that good soul. It is too raunchy, too crazy, too strange. Scenes like that in which the Scapehouse sisters eat stuffed kitten while Bigfoot crouches under the table performing cunnilingus on them, or in which Bigfoot decapitates the man who has stolen the bronze statue he is in love with, or in which the cripples tear Little Big Mouse limb from limb, are too bizarre and painful for the "common reader." Post-modern fiction, as Stevick puts it, "willingly acknowledges the partiality of its truth, the oddity of its vision, and the limits of its audience."[20]

Third, *Bearheart,* like other post-modern novels, incorporates generous amounts of bad art. It is an irony that new fiction, caviar to the general, borrows much from the art of the masses. This is not new to literature: a New York Irish barroom song is at the heart of *Finnegan's Wake,* and Ionesco, when asked about the major influence on his work, named Groucho, Chico, and Harpo Marx. But if this tendency predates the new fiction, it is carried to new highs —or lows—there. Ishmael Reed works Minnie the Moocher and Amos and Andy into *The Last Days of Louisiana Red,* and Alvin Greenberg's *Invention of the West* is based on the schlock Western novel and horse opera. Although greatly transcending them, *Bearheart* has certain similarities in tone, subject, and approach to *Mad* and *Penthouse* magazines and to Andy Warhol movies like *Frankenstein.*

Stevick points out that, although we are oblivious to and therefore unoffended by the Irish popular culture in Joyce's work, the popular art in the new fiction is our own bad art, and we recognize and deplore it. As Stevick puts it, new fiction seems more "audacious and abrasive than it really is because it occupies a place at what William Gass, following Barthelme, calls the 'leading edge of the trash phenomenon.'"[21]

As for philosophical and aesthetic depth, *Bearheart* is as devoid of it as are the works of Barthelme, Reed, and Elkin. In contrast to writers like Momaday, who makes heavy use of symbolism, novelists like Vizenor eschew it completely. For them the surface is the meaning; there is nothing between the lines but white space, as Barthelme says.[22]

I hardly need to belabor Stevick's point that new fiction departs from the illusionist tradition. Obviously *Bearheart* is a radical departure from the air of reality that James admires in novels. What Vizenor is doing is creating a caricature by exaggerating tendencies already present in American culture, so that even if the picture he paints is grotesque or not at all true to life, it is recognizable, like a newspaper cartoon of Jimmy Carter or Ronald Reagan.

Finally, the post-modern novel is writing as play. There are precedents for this, of course: Laurence Sterne's *Tristram Shandy* comes to mind, and undoubtedly Joyce was playing in *Finnegan's Wake*, though the joke seems to be on the reader. The tone of *Bearheart* may be at times savage, bitter, or violent, but at the heart of the book is an ever-present and peculiarly Indian sense of humor.

Whites may wonder just what it is that Indians have to laugh about today, or they may psychologize about the Indians' need for laughter, but this is unfair to Indians, who, despite the dour image of the cigar-store mannikin, have always cherished humor for its own sake. Vizenor has a story in *Wordarrows* about how the U.S. Communist Party's secretary general, Gus Hall, asked protesting Indians in Minneapolis to write about their grievances for communist newspapers. Vizenor states: "The tribal protest committee refused to write for the communists because— in addition to political reasons—there was too little humor in communist speech, making it impossible to know the heart of the speakers."[23]

Bearheart shocks and puzzles many readers, but once it is understood that Vizenor's fiction is shaped by Anishinabe folklore and the post-modern tradition, the book is not so puzzling after all.

Earthdivers, Vizenor's latest book, is about mixed-bloods.[24] In this work Vizenor (who, like Silko, is keenly aware of being half-white and half-Indian) tries to celebrate the unique status of the mixed-bloods—to reverse the prejudice that has plagued them, to make a hero of the half-breed. To appreciate what Vizenor does, it is useful to review racial attitudes toward Indians and mixed-bloods in America.

The word *half-breed* has always had a negative connotation in American English, like *half-blood*, it seems to connote bastardy. Mixed descent is not necessarily bad; Oklahoma politicians, and most other Oklahomans, for that matter, are eager enough to claim Indian blood. But the figure of the half-blood in the racist mythology of the Old West often represented an illicit mixture of the worst of both races, the hateful, untrustworthy spawn of renegades and barmaids.

According to Harold Beaver, John Rolfe was the first British colonist to marry an Indian, a woman named Motsoaks'ats.[25] Their son, Thomas Rolfe, would appear to have the distinction of being the first American mixed-blood. Although the colonists were aware of the Biblical prohibition about marrying "strange wives" and passed laws against intermarriage between whites and Indians, the practice was widespread, and mixed-bloods like Sequoyah, Osceola, Stand Watie, and Jesse Chisholm were famous—or infamous, depending on one's politics—in the nineteenth century.

Mixed-blood characters in American fiction are generally negative, or at best ambiguous; Injun Joe of *Tom Sawyer,* for instance, is a "half breed devil." Twain, who was so compassionate to blacks, revealed a great deal of intolerance in his depictions of Indians, not only in *Tom Sawyer* but also in his account of the "Goshoot Indians" in *Roughing It.* His hideous portrait of Injun Joe seems to indicate a belief that, if full bloods were backwards, half-breeds were bestial.

138

Beaver lists other literary mixed-bloods who appear in major American literary works—Poe's Dirk Peters *(The Narrative of Arthur Gordon Pym)*, Hemingway's Dick Boulton *(In Our Time)*, and Faulkner's Boon Hogganbeck and Sam Fathers *(Go Down Moses)*—and states that "all are pariahs in some sense—quick-witted, tough, valiant even—who are revealed as the ambiguous saviors of white men."[26] To this list we might add Ken Kesey's Broom Bronden of *One Flew over the Cuckoo's Nest,* who, though certainly not quick-witted, is a pariah and who, in a highly ambiguous sense, saves Randle Patrick McMurphy from what he perceives as a fate worse than death, life as a vegetable.

Racial attitudes change quickly, and today white Americans' ideas about mixed-bloods are a subset of their ideas about Indians, and these need to be briefly reviewed, and in particular contrasted to, their ideas about other minorities, especially blacks. In the chapter "The Red and the Black" in *Custer Died for Your Sins,* Vine Deloria points out that Indians and blacks were treated not only differently, but with an opposite emphasis: blacks were systematically excluded from white American life, while Indians were forced into it:

> It is well to keep these distinctions clearly in mind when talking about Indians and blacks. When liberals equate the two they are overlooking obvious historical facts. Never did the white man systematically exclude Indians from his schools and meeting places. Nor did the government ever kidnap black children from their homes and take them off to a government boarding school to be educated as whites. . . . The white man systematically destroyed Indian culture where it existed, but separated blacks from his midst so that they were forced to attempt the creation of their own culture. . . . The white man forbade the black to enter his own social and economic system, and at the same time force-fed the Indian what he was denying the black.[27]

Whatever progress in integration of blacks has been made

in the past decade, the legacy of segregation remains, and the point is still valid.

Perceptive as his essay is, Deloria omits two points that have an important bearing on our perception of mixed-bloods. The first is that you can be half Indian, but you cannot be half black; if you are discernibly black, you are black, period. During slavery, when blacks were sold, distinctions were made between *mulattos, quadroons,* and *octaroons,* and the term *mulatto* was current in American speech in my youth. Whether because of black pride or some other factor, there is no such word any more: *mulatto* is a signifier without a signified. The coffee-colored O. J. Simpson is a black, or an Afro-American perhaps, but he is definitely not a mulatto.

Contrarily, a mixed-blood with one full-blood grandparent, with one-quarter Indian "blood," is considered presumptuous, mendacious in fact, if he claims that he is simply Indian. Whereas light-skinned products of black-white marriages are accorded the same sort of treatment as their darker brothers, the lighter progeny of Indian-white marriages are often derided by whites if they try to claim tribal identity. "You are not an Indian; you're one of us" is what mixed-bloods are told, even in cases in which they have an Indian name.

The rules for ethnic identity vary with the group. You are a Jew only if your mother is a Jew or if you convert, and among the orthodox your gentile mother must convert, too (a hangover from the days when men were more suspicious of their wives and when Cossacks raped Jewish girls). The mainstream American attitude toward ethnicity is that you are what your father is, that is, what your name is. If your name is Kowalski, you are Polish, even if your mother's name is O'Brien or Goldberg. Nor are you asked to prove that you are Polish. Finally, Indians are the only racial group, with the exception of WASPs, that anyone ever tries to sneak into. I have never heard of anyone who tried to pass for black, or Jewish, or Italian, but I know a number of cases in which whites have tried to pass for Indians.

White attitudes toward Indian mixed-bloods are more hostile in literature and film than they are in life. In Oklahoma, for instance, the Cherokee Indian blood of Will Rogers and W. W. Keeler (former president and chairman of the board of Phillips Petroleum Company) was regarded as a positive, romantic, and colorful attribute. Keeler, who was elected principal chief of the Cherokees, was proud of his Indian blood and received a great deal of publicity as a result of it.

Vizenor comes from a corner of the country where mixed-bloods have a sense of identity of their own. He is a Minnesota Métis. *Métis* is a French word (cognate with Spanish *mestizo*) for a person of mixed Indian and French-Canadian ancestry. Whether it was because these whites were Gallic rather than English, Catholic rather than Protestant, or nomadic trappers rather than sedentary, land-hungry farmers, the French Canadians were more tolerant of the Indians than were the Anglo-Americans, and married with them more frequently. The result was the Métis, a mixed-blood people with a definite cultural identity. Vizenor quotes historian Jacqueline Peterson: "Intermarriage went hand in glove with the trade in skins and furs from the first decades of discovery. . . . The core denominator of Métis identity was not participation in the fur-trading network per se, but the mixed-blood middleman stance between Indian and European societies."[28] Because Vizenor's family were Anishinabes from the White Earth Reservation, and his mother was a Beaulieu, he is Métis in the narrow as well as the extended sense of the term, which now simply means mixed-blood.

Vizenor's central metaphor for mixed-bloods is the earth-diver of the Anishinabe creation myth. This myth, which appears in many cultures throughout the world, has four invariable traits: a world covered with water, a creator, a diver, and the creation of land. The Anishinabe version, in which the trickster Wenebojo is the diver, goes as follows: Wenebojo is on top of a tree that is protruding from the water. He defecates, and his excrement floats to the top. He asks Otter to dive to the bottom and bring up some dirt out of which to construct the earth. Otter tries but drowns. Wenebojo revives him and asks him if he saw any dirt, but Otter says "no." Next Wenebojo asks Beaver, who also drowns. When revived, Beaver says that he saw some dirt, but could not get to it. Then Muskrat tries. He too floats to the surface, senseless, but clenched in his paws and in his mouth are five grains of sand. Wenebojo revives Muskrat and throws the sand into the water, forming a small island. Wenebojo gets more dirt, enlarging the island, and lives there with the animals.

Psychologizing anthropologists explain this tale as a cloacal myth, that is, as one that reflects male envy of female pregnancy in its excremental theory of creation. It is typical of Vizenor's sense of irony that he both presents and ridicules the theory of excremental creation. It is always hard to pin Vizenor down. He seems to give credence to the idea, which he finds amusing, but deplores the "secular seriousness" of the scholars who propose it: "The academic intensities of career-bound anthropologists approach diarrhetic levels of terminal theoretical creeds" (p. 12).

The earthdiver is Vizenor's central metaphor for the mixed-blood. The vehicle *earthdiver* has two elements, the earth and the diver. As a diver the mixed-blood cuts through the polluted sea we live in to the rich floor below, and brings back some earth to create a new land:

White settlers are summoned to dive with mixed-blood survivors into the unknown, into the legal morass of treaties and bureaucratic evils, and to swim deep down and around through federal exclaves and colonial economic enterprises in search of a few honest words upon which to build a new urban turtle island. [P. 7]

The earth, the other part of the vehicle, not only signifies nature, the sacred earth, but also federal funds, the rich muck that acts like manure on tribal projects:

> When the mixed-blood earthdiver summons the white world to dive like the otter and beaver and muskrat in search of the earth, and federal funds, he is both animal and trickster, both white and tribal, the uncertain creator in an urban metaphor based on a creation myth that preceded him in two world views and oral tradition. [P. 15]

And, as a metaphor yokes two different things in one comparison, mixed-bloods are linked between white and tribal cultures: "Métis earthdivers are the new metaphors between communal tribal cultures and those cultures which oppose traditional connections, the cultures which would market the earth" (p. 18). All of Vizenor's mixed-bloods are earthdivers of one kind or another, but the story of Martin Bear Charme corresponds best to the earthdiver myth as a cloacal creation story. A founder of the Landfill Meditation Reservation, Bear Charme pops up in a number of Vizenor's works.

Bear Charme left his reservation in North Dakota and hitchhiked to San Francisco when he was sixteen. He tried welding in a federal relocation program but soon turned to garbage, out of which he built his fortune, "hauling trash and filling wet lands with solid waste and urban swill" in the South Bay area. Having made his life out of refuse, Bear Charme, unlike other scraplords who went from dumps to mansions, made garbage his life, meditating in his dump, and seeing garbage as a metaphor for the worthwhile things in life—contact with the earth, and the process of recycling and renewal.

With Bear Charme, Vizenor stands a cliché on its head.

We normally think of filling the Bay as despoiling nature—
that is certainly the way conservation-oriented newspapers
like the *Bay Guardian* portray it—but Vizenor, with his
characteristic irony, shows that making land from garbage
is a reverential act to nature:

> The status of a trash hauler is one of the best measures
> of how separated a culture is from the earth, from the
> smell of its own waste. Bear Charme teaches that we should
> turn our minds back to the earth, the rich smell of the
> titled earth. We are the garbage he [once said]. We are
> the real waste, and cannot separate ourselves like machines,
> clean and dumped, trashed out back into the river. We are
> the earthdiver and dreamers, and the holistic waste. [P.
> 136]

Bear Charme makes his dump a "meditation reservation,"
a place to renew one's link to the earth:

> Charme chanted *"come to the landfill and focus on real
> waste,"* shaman crow crowed backward on her perch in the
> sumac. *"Mandala mulch, and transcend the grammatical
> word rivers, clean talk and terminal creeds,* and put mind
> back to earth. Dive back to the earth, *come backward to
> meditate on trash, and swill and real* waste that binds us
> to our bodies and the earth. [P. 131]

One of the appealing things about Vizenor's works is
that they appear to be one huge moebius strip. Never mind
that there are poems, essays, stories, and novels. They seem
to be parts of a unified whole because the same characters
scuttle in and out, often telling the same stories. Rattling
Hail appears in a poem and then an essay; Lilith Mae
Farrier is in an essay and then a novel; Clement Beaulieu
appears everywhere. Bear Charme first appeared in a story
entitled "Land Fill Meditation," which was published in the
Minneapolis Star Saturday Magazine in February, 1979. In
the story, Beaulieu/Vizenor introduced Bear Charme as the
narrator who tells the story of Belladonna Darwin-Winter

Catcher, the mixed-blood killed for her terminal views. Vizenor lifts the tale, without Bear Charme, and puts it in *Darkness in Saint Louis Bearheart.* The story appears a third time in "Windmills of Dwinelle Hall," an episode in *Fourskin,* Vizenor's unpublished novel about life in the Native American Studies Department at Berkeley. The story is narrated by Bear Charme, a character in "Landfill Meditation," a collection of stories by Clement Beaulieu, alias Gerald Vizenor. These stories are the subject of a seminar conducted by Pink Stallion, a key *schlussel* in this *roman à clef,* a mixed-blood Valentino known for picking the lock of every blonde in Berkeley.

The narrative technique of "Windmills" is marvelous, a *mise en abime* in which Vizenor is the oat box Quaker holding up a box on which Pink Stallion is seen holding up a box on which Beaulieu/Vizenor is seen holding up a box on which Bear Charme is seen telling the story of Belladonna Darwin-Winter Catcher. This story, slightly revised, appears as "Classroom Windmills" in *Earthdivers.*

In the Anishinabe myth the earthdiver is the trickster Wenebojo. As the product of the marriage between a spirit and a man, Wenebojo is a sort of mixed-blood himself. In Anishinabe mythology, and indeed, all Indian mythology, the trickster is mediator between man and god, a hero sent by God (Manito, Earthmaker, Wakan Tanka) to help man on earth. In a way the mixed-blood is a mediator as well: most Indian Studies programs are staffed by mixed-bloods, who become interpreters who define tribal culture to the white community.

The trickster in Vizenor's work who best captures the spirit of Anishinabe mythology is one who operates in the academic arena, Captain Shammer, the short-term chairman of American Indian Studies at Berkeley in *Earthdivers.* Shammer, called Captain because he is a trickster of martial masks who parades around campus as a military man, was selected as the seventh chairman of American Indian Studies because he had the fewest credentials and was lowest on the list of applicants. The search committee reasoned that the past six chairs, who had failed miserably, were experts, and that it was time to pick someone without qualifications. Shammer, true to his military nature, "took hold of the well-worn pink plastic mixed-blood reins and rode the old red wagon constellations proud as a tribal trickster through the ancient word wars, with mule skinners and ruminant mammals, behind academic lines" (p. 25).

Shammer's term lasts three weeks—tricksters, as I said, are traditionally peripatetic—but during those weeks he has an enormous impact. His first move is to put the Department of American Indian Studies up for sale to the highest bidder. This may seem outrageous, but as Dean Colin Defender puts it, "Higher education has always been for sale on both ends, research and instruction; the difference here is that this new Chair, part cracker I might add, is seeking the highest, not the lowest, bids." The winner of the bidding is the Committee on Tribal Indecision, which changes the name of the department to Undecided Studies.

Another service that Captain Shammer performs for his department is to bring in Old Darkhorse, proprietor of the *Half Moon Bay Skin Dip*, whose specialty is coloring skin. Now America's attitude about skin color is not simple. On the one hand, light skin is better than dark when it serves to identify a person as Caucasian rather than Indian or black. Being pale, however, is inferior to being tan the color of the leisure class of Aspen and Acapulco. As long as one is easily identifiable as a Caucasian, it is good to be as dark as possible. Lightness is also a disadvantage for mixed-bloods, both among tribal people and among members of the white community (who can feel more liberal if they are dealing with dark dark people and not wasting their liberalism on light dark people). Accordingly, Old Darkhorse performs a real service by darkening mixed-bloods through dunking. In his early experiments the technology was not very sophisticated, and the dunkees would emerge "marbled . . . like the end papers on old books" (p. 47). Soon, however, Darkhorse perfects his process and is able to help light mixed-bloods "when the darkest mixed-bloods were much too critical of the light inventions, the pale skins varieties needed darker flesh to disburden their lack of confidence around white liberals" (p. 46).

One of the main thrusts of the "satirical contradance" Shammer performs is Vizenor's spoof of Americans' reactions to skin color—not only the prejudices of whites but those of mixed-bloods and full bloods as well. Vizenor is well aware that no race has a monopoly on prejudice, and he has no reluctance to satirize the color consciousness of Indians. To this end he has Captain Shammer introduce his colorwheel, a register of skin tones ranging from white through pink and tan to dark brown. The colors are numbered and refer to explanations in a manual on tribal skin tones and identities. Shammer, for instance, was a four, about which the manual reads:

> Mixedbloods with the skin tone color wheel code four are too mixed to choose absolute breeds or terminal creeds. Fours are too light to dance in the traditional tribal world and too dark to escape their flesh in the white world . . . . Fours bear the potential to be four flushers, too much white in the hand and not enough in the tribal bush. [P. 43]

Having darkened the pale mixed-bloods and sold the department, Shammer moves on, trickster fashion.

In all his works, but most of all in *Earthdivers,* Vizenor deals with the delicate subjects of race relations, color, and ethnic identity. But he does not deal with them delicately. He slashes away at prejudices and "terminal beliefs" with merciless satire, exposing and ridiculing whites, full bloods, and mixed-bloods. His friends are no safer than his enemies, and being on his side does not guarantee immunity from being lampooned. That is the way it should be, of course, and, as much as anyone, Gerald Vizenor deserves a place in the Half-Breed Hall of Fame.

NOTES

Preface

1. Alan Dundes, *Analytical Essays in Folklore* (Hawthorne, N.Y.: Mouton Publishers, 1975).
2. Alan R. Velie, ed., *American Indian Literature: An Anthology* (Norman: University of Oklahoma Press, 1979).

Chapter 1

1. Al Young, "A Dance for Militant Dilettantes," in *Dancing* (New Haven, Conn.: Corinth Press, 1969).
2. James Welch, "The Only Good Indian," *South Dakota Review* 9 (1971): 54.
3. James Baldwin, "Everybody's Protest Novel," in *Notes of a Native Son* (Boston: Beacon Press, 1955), p. 54.
4. Ibid., p. 22.
5. Ibid., p. 19.
6. Ishmael Reed, *19 Necromancers from Now* (Garden City, N.Y.: Doubleday, Anchor Books, 1970), p. xii.

Chapter 2

1. N. Scott Momaday, *The Names* (New York: Harper and Row, 1976), p. 150; all subsequent references are to this edition.

2. N. Scott Momaday, *The Way to Rainy Mountain* (Albuquerque, N.Mex.: University of New Mexico Press, 1969), p. 80.

3. Ibid., p. 52.

4. Malcolm Cowley, *Exile's Return* (New York: Viking Press, 1964), p. 13.

5. *Santa Fe New Mexican,* November 5, 1972.

6. Kenneth Fields, "More than Language Means," *Southern Review* 6 (Winter, 1970): 196-204.

7. The work of this important turn-of-the-century scholar includes *The Ghost Dance Religion and the Sioux Outbreak of 1890,* Smithsonian Institution, Bureau of American Ethnology Fourteenth Annual Report (Washington, D.C., 1896) and *Calendar History of the Kiowa Indians* (1898; reprint, Washington, D.C.: Smithsonian Institution Press, 1980).

8. N. Scott Momaday, "A Few Thoughts About Buffalo," *Santa Fe New Mexican,* March 18, 1973.

9. N. Scott Momaday, *House Made of Dawn* (New York: New American Library, Signet Books, 1969), p. 89.

10. Natachee Momaday, *American Indian Authors* (Boston: Houghton Mifflin, 1972), p. 3.

11. A. Grove Day, *The Sky Clears* (Lincoln: University of Nebraska Press, 1951), p. 2.

Chapter 3

1. N. Scott Momaday, ed., *The Complete Poems of Frederick Goddard Tuckerman* (New York: Oxford University Press, 1965).

2. For a full discussion of post-symbolism, see Yvor Winters, *Forms of Discovery: Critical and Historical Essays on the Forms of the Short Poem in English* (Denver: Alan Swallow, 1967), p. 251 ff.

3. Howard Kaye, "The Post-Symbolist Poetry of Yvor Winters," *The Southern Review* 7, no. 1 (January, 1971): 176-97.

4. Winters, *Forms,* p. 251.

5. Kaye, "Post-Symbolist Poetry," p. 180.

6. N. Scott Momaday, *The Gourd Dancer* (New York: Harper and Row, 1976), p. 31.

7. *Santa Fe New Mexican,* September 23, 1973, p. 13.

8. Winters, *Forms,* p. 289.

9. Yvor Winters, "To William Dinsmore Briggs Conducting His Seminar," in *Collected Poems* (Denver: Alan Swallow, 1960), p. 47.

10. Momaday, "The Bear," in *Gourd Dancer,* p. 11.

11. See Kenneth Roemer, "Bear and Elk: The Nature(s) of Contemporary Indian Poetry," *Journal of Ethnic Studies* 5, no. 2 (Summer, 1977): 69-79.

12. William Faulkner, "The Bear," in *Go Down, Moses* (New York: Random House, Modern Library, 1942), p. 209.

13. Winters, *Forms,* p. 290.

14. Ibid.

15. In his foreword to Momaday's *Complete Poems of Frederick Goddard Tuckerman,* Winters says that "Wordsworth, the poet of nature, popularized nature, but almost never saw it; his descriptions are almost always stereotypes."

16. Winters, *Forms,* p. 290.

17. Momaday, "Buteo Regalis," in *Gourd Dancer,* p. 72.

18. Winters, *Forms,* p. 291.

19. Momaday, *Complete Poems of Tuckerman,* p. xxvi.

20. Ibid., p. xvi. Winters, with his characteristic hyperbole, calls Tuckerman's poem "The Cricket" the greatest poem in English of the nineteenth century.

21.   Flower in the crannied wall,
          I pluck you out of the crannies,
          I hold you here, root and all, in my hand,
          Little flower—but if I could understand
          What you are, root and all, and all in all,
          I should know what God and man is.

22. "The Heretical Cricket," *Southern Review* 3, nos. 1-2 (1967): 43-50.

23. Momaday, *Gourd Dancer,* p. 28.

24. Another poem worth comparing to "Before an Old Picture" is Wallace Stevens's "Sunday Morning." Stevens was one of the poets Winters included among the post-symbolists, and one whose work Momaday was certainly familiar with. "Sunday Morning" starts with an allusion to the crucifixion: a woman dreams of the "ancient sacrifice, . . . that old catastrophe." As in "Before an Old Picture," God is dead, and the woman asks why she should

"give her bounty to the dead?" The attitude of the poem is a hedonistic form of existentialism: divinity should be sought in "comforts of the sun . . . or else / In a balm or beauty of the earth," in fact, all passions, not only pleasant but "all pleasures and all pains."

Both poems deal with the problems of death and what is alluded to in poetry as "mutability"—that is, the ravages of time. Momaday, although troubled by the passage of time, nonetheless describes the timeless, "endless afternoon" of the mural as a scene of "sterile loveliness." Stevens makes the same point more emphatically. In the passage that begins, "Death is the mother of beauty," he asks, "Is there no change of death in paradise? / Does ripe fruit never fall?" The point, as in Keats's "Ode to Melancholy," is that without death there is no fulfillment.

25. Momaday, *Complete Poems of Tuckerman*, p. 69.
26. Momaday, *Gourd Dancer*, pp. 25, 41.

Chapter 4

1. Charles Woodard is a professor of English at South Dakota State University. At the time of the interview he was a graduate student at the University of Oklahoma, working on his dissertation, "The Concept of the Creative Word in the Writings of N. Scott Momaday" (1975). The interview has not been published.
2. N. Scott Momaday, *House Made of Dawn* (New York: New American Library, 1969), p. 49; all subsequent quotes are from this edition.
3. H. S. McAllister, "Incarnate Grace and the Paths of Salvation in *House Made of Dawn*," *American Indian Quarterly* 2, no. 1 (Spring 1975): 14-22.
4. Herman Melville, *Moby Dick* (Boston: Houghton Mifflin, 1956), p. 163.
5. Ibid., p. 160.
6. Woodard: "Is there anything Melvillian about him? The ambiguity of his color?" Momaday: "Yes. I don't know how far I would go with that, but yes, I certainly had that in mind when I was writing."
7. Momaday, *House Made of Dawn*, p. 85 ff.

8. See N. Scott Momaday, *The Names* (New York: Harper and Row, 1976), p. 128. According to Butler's *Lives of the Saints*, Saint Didacus, or Diego, was a Spanish monk (d. 1463) from Seville. Butler gives his day as November 13.

9. See, for instance, Paul Radin, *The Trickster: A Study in American Indian Mythology* (Westport, Conn.: Greenwood Press, 1956), p. 111 ff.

Chapter 5

1. James Welch, *Riding the Earthboy Forty*, rev. ed. (New York: Harper and Row, 1975). The first edition was favorably reviewed in the *Saturday Review* of October 2, 1971, but World Publishing Company allowed it to go out of print. Harper and Row published the revised edition with seven new poems. Welch has attracted some attention in Europe; Roswith von Freydorf Riese, a German poet and critic from Heidelberg, has been translating his poems.

2. I am gratefully indebted to my colleague Madison Morrison for explaining Welch's surrealism to me.

3. Anna Balakian, *Surrealism: The Road to the Absolute* (New York: E. P. Dutton, 1970), p. 128.

4. Ibid., p. 151.

5. Ibid., p. 152.

6. Ibid., p. 145.

7. Robert Bly, ed., *Seventies No. 1: An Anthology of Leaping Poetry* (Berkeley, Calif.: Seventies Press, 1972), p. 30.

8. Ibid., p. 11.

9. Robert Bly, ed., *Neruda and Vallejo: Selected Poems* (Boston: Beacon Press, 1971), p. 175.

10. Ibid., "Poem to Be Read and Sung," p. 247.

11. Ibid., "And What If After So Many Words," p. 263.

12. Ibid., "Have You Anything to Say in Your Defense?" p. 217.

13. Ibid., "The Weary Circles," p. 207.

14. James Wright, *Collected Poems* (Middletown, Conn.: Wesleyan University Press, 1971), p. 154.

15. Ibid., "Two Poems about President Harding," p. 120.

16. Ibid., "At the Executioner's Grave," p. 82.

17. Ibid., "St. Judas," p. 84.
18. Ibid., "In the Face of Hatred," p. 114.
19. Ibid., "A Message Hidden in an Empty Wine Bottle. . . ,"
p. 115.
20. Welch, *Riding*, p. 3.
21. T. S. Eliot, "Dante," in *Selected Essays* (New York: Harcourt Brace Jovanovich, 1950).
22. Welch, *Riding*, p. 6.
23. Ibid., p. 12.
24. George Bird Grinnell, *Blackfoot Lodge Tales* (Lincoln: University of Nebraska Press, 1962), p. 192.
25. Welch, *Riding*, p. 53.
26. James Welch, quoted in the *South Dakota Review* 9, no. 2 (Summer, 1971): 54.
27. Welch, *Riding*, p. 18. The comment about the Mormons seems to deserve explication. My assumption is that Welch is referring to the "placement program," in which Mormon families "adopt" Indian children of school age during the school year; during summers the children—mostly Navajos—return to the reservation.
28. Ibid., p. 34.
29. Ibid., p. 64.
30. Ibid., p. 27.
31. See, for instance, Alexander Henry and David Thompson, *New Light on The Early History of the Greater Northwest* (New York: F. P. Harper, 1897), II:306.

Chapter 6

1. Blanche H. Gelfant, for example, says that *Winter in the Blood* is about the "death of a people" and that "we must read it to our despair." She blames the narrator's troubles on his "bruised and defeated spirit," the result of white oppression. Nowhere does she mention the humor in the novel. See her "Fiction Chronicle," *Hudson Review* 28 (Summer, 1975): 311-12.
2. James Welch, *Riding the Earthboy Forty*, rev. ed. (New York: Harper and Row, 1975), pp. 25, 30.
3. "De fabula," in Paul Wesner, ed., *Aeli Donati quod fertur*

commentium Terenti (Leipzig, 1902-1908), vol. 1, p. 62 (author's translation).

4. Ibid., p. 60.

5. What do we call novels that are not comic? There is a paucity of terms. "Tragic novel" is seldom heard, though novels like *Tess of the D'Urbervilles* and *For Whom the Bell Tolls* are clearly tragic. "Serious novel" is not satisfactory, for comedy can be serious too. And no writer would want his novel to be called "solemn."

6. Northrop Frye, *Anatomy of Criticism* (Princeton, N.J.: Princeton University Press, 1957), p. 34.

7. Ibid., p. 41.

8. James Welch, *Winter in the Blood* (New York: Harper and Row, 1974), p. 1; all subsequent quotations are from this edition.

9. *New York Times Book Review*, November 10, 1974, p. 1.

10. Professor Michael Dorris advanced this view at a meeting of teachers of Indian literature, sponsored by the Modern Language Association, held at Southern Methodist University in October, 1976.

Chapter 7

1. Quoted in Kenneth Rosen, *The Man to Send Rain Clouds* (New York: Random House, Vintage Books, 1975), p. 176.

2. Florence Ellis, *Anthropology of Laguna Pueblo Land Claims* (New York: Garland, 1974), p. 1.

3. Ibid., p. 5.

4. From Kenneth Rosen, *Voices of the Rainbow* (New York: Viking Press, 1975), p. 230

5. Leslie Silko, *Laguna Woman* (Greenfield, N.Y.: Greenfield Review Press, 1974); many of her best short stories are included in Rosen, *Man to Send Rain Clouds.*

6. Quoted from the dust jacket of Leslie Silko, *Ceremony* (New York: Viking Press, 1977); all subsequent quotations are from this edition.

7. Silko told me this in a telephone conversation of February 3, 1978.

8. See Jessie L. Weston, *From Ritual to Romance* (Cam-

bridge: At the University Press, 1920), chap. 2.

9. Edmund Wilson, *Axel's Castle* (New York: Scribner's, 1953), p. 106.

10. F. Scott Fitzgerald, *The Great Gatsby* (New York: Scribner's, 1953), p. 149.

11. Weston, *From Ritual*, p. 23.

12. Wayne C. Booth, *The Rhetoric of Fiction* (Chicago: University of Chicago Press, 1961), p. 71.

13. Ellis, *Anthropology*, p. 18.

14. Silko to the author, February 3, 1978.

15. Translated by Jessie Weston in *From Ritual*, p. 106.

Chapter 8

1. Both *Chippewa* and *Ojibwa* are transliterations of a word for a type of moccasin worn by the tribe that had an unusual puckered seam (*ojib-ubway*, "to roast until puckered up"). *Anishinabe* means "original or first man." See Frances Densmore, *Chippewa Customs*, Smithsonian Institution, Bureau of American Ethnology Bulletin no. 86 (Washington, D.C., 1929), p. 5.

2. See Gerald Vizenor, "I Know What You Mean, Erdupps MacChurbbs: Autobiographical Myths and Metaphors," in *Growing Up in Minnesota* (Minneapolis: University of Minnesota Press, 1975), p. 81 ff.

3. Kenneth Rosen, ed., *Voices of the Rainbow* (New York: Viking Press, 1975).

4. Vizenor, "I Know What You Mean," p. 95.

5. Gerald Vizenor, *Wordarrows: Indians and Whites in the New Fur Trade* (Minneapolis: University of Minnesota Press, 1978).

6. Rosen, *Voices*, p. 42.

7. Ibid., p. 32.

8. For a full discussion of the Trickster figures in Indian and other mythology, see Paul Radin, *The Trickster: A Study in American Indian Mythology* (Westport, Conn.: Greenwood Press, 1956).

9. William Jones and Truman Michelson, eds., *Ojibway Texts* (Leyden: E. J. Brill, 1917) and Basil Johnson, *Ojibway Heritage* (New York: Columbia University Press, 1976).

10. Jones and Michelson, *Ojibway Texts,* p. 17 ff.

11. Ibid., p. 279 ff.

12. Barbara Tedlock, "The Clown's Way," in Dennis and Barbara Tedlock, *Teachings from the American Earth* (New York: W. W. Norton, Liveright, 1975), p. 105 ff.

13. B. Tedlock, "Clown's Way," p. 115.

14. See Melville Jacobs, *Content and Style of an Oral Literature: Clackamas Chinook Myths and Tales* (Chicago: University of Chicago Press, 1959), p. 37 ff.

15. Vizenor has assured me that the Chippewas have an Evil Gambler figure.

16. Leslie Marmon Silko, *Ceremony,* p. 170 ff.

17. Zebulon Matchi Makwa is also a friend of Vizenor's who appears in *Wordarrows,* and Mean Nettles of "I Know What You Mean" appears in part of a story that Iniwa Biwide tells.

18. Henry James, *The Future of the Novel* (New York: Vintage Books, 1956), pp. 5, 14.

19. Phillip Stevick, "Scherezade Runs Out of Plots. . . ," *Triquarterly* 26 (Winter, 1973): 332-62.

20. Ibid., p. 355.

21. Ibid., p. 356.

22. Ibid., p. 360.

23. Vizenor, *Wordarrows,* p. 17.

24. Gerald Vizenor, *Earthdivers: Tribal Narratives on Mixed Descent* (Minneapolis: University of Minnesota Press, 1981).

25. Harold Beaver, "On the Racial Frontier," *Times Literary Supplement,* 30 May 1980, p. 619.

26. Ibid., p. 619.

27. Vine Deloria, Jr., *Custer Died for Your Sins* (New York: Avon Books, 1970), p. 173.

28. Vizenor, *Earthdivers,* p. 6. Subsequent page references are to *Earthdivers.*

SELECTED BIBLIOGRAPHY

N. Scott Momaday

Barry, Nora Baker. "The Bear's Son Folk Tale in *When the Legends Die* and *House Made of Dawn*." *Western American Literature* 12 (1978):275-87.

Bloodworth, William. "Neihardt, Momaday, and the Art of Indian Autobiography." In *Where the West Begins: Essays on Middle Border and Siouxland Writings, in Honor of Herbert Krause,* ed. Arthur R. Huseboe and William Geyer. Sioux Falls, Idaho: Center for Western Studies, Augustana College, 1978.

Davis, Jack L. "The Whorf Hypothesis and Native American Literature." *South Dakota Review* 12 (1976):115-25.

Dickinson-Brown, Roger. "The Art and Importance of N. Scott Momaday." *Southern Review* 14(1978):30-45.

Evers, Lawrence J. "Words and Place: A Reading of *House Made of Dawn*." *Western American Literature* 11(1977):297-320.

Hylton, Marion W. "On a Trail of Pollen: Momaday's *House Made of Dawn*." *Critique* 14(1972):60-79.

Kerr, Baine. "The Novel as Sacred Text: N. Scott Momaday's Myth-Making Ethic." *Southwest Review* 63(1978):172-79.

Larson, Charles R. *American Indian Fiction*. Albuquerque: University of New Mexico Press, 1978.

McAllister, Harold S. "Be a Man, Be a Woman: Androgyny in *House Made of Dawn*." *American Indian Quarterly* 2(1976): 14-44.

———. "Incarnate Grace and the Paths of Salvation in *House*

Made of Dawn." *South Dakota Review* 12(1972):115-25.

———. "The Topology of Remembrance in *The Way to Rainy Mountain.*" *Denver Quarterly* 12(1978):19-31.

Nicholas, Charles A. "The Way to Rainy Mountain: N. Scott Momaday's Hard Journey Back." *South Dakota Review* 13 (1975):149-58.

Oleson, Carole. "The Remembered Earth: Momaday's House Made of Dawn." *South Dakota Review* 11(1973):59-78.

Roemer, Kenneth M. "Bear and Elk: The Nature(s) of Contemporary Indian Poetry." *Journal of Ethnic Studies* 5(1977):69-79.

———. "Survey Courses, Indian Literature, and *The Way to Rainy Mountain.*" *College English* 37(1976):619-24.

Strelke, Barbara. "N. Scott Momaday: Racial Memory and Individual Imagination." In *Literature of the American Indians: Views and Interpretations: A Gathering of Indian Memories, Symbolic Contexts and Literary Criticism,* ed. Abraham Chapman. New York: New American Library, 1975.

Trimble, Martha S. *N. Scott Momaday.* Western Writers Service no. 9. Boise, Idaho: Boise State College. 46 pp.

Trimmer, Joseph F. "Native Americans and the American Mix: N. Scott Momaday's *House Made of Dawn.*" *Indiana Social Studies Quarterly* 28(1975):75-91.

Woodard, Charles L. "Momaday's *House Made of Dawn.*" *Explicator* 36(1978):27-28.

Young, Jim. "Tradition and the Experimental." *Compass* 1(1977): 99-107.

Zachrau, Thekla. "N. Scott Momaday: Towards an Indian Identity." *Dutch Quarterly Review of Anglo-American Letters* 9(1979): 52-70.

James Welch

Barnett, Louise K. "Alienation and Ritual in *Winter in the Blood.*" *American Indian Quarterly* 4(1978):123-30.

Barry, Nora Baker. "*Winter in the Blood* as Elegy." *American Indian Quarterly* 4(1978):149-57.

Beidler, Peter G., ed. "A Special Symposium Issue on James

Welch's *Winter in the Blood.*" *American Indian Quarterly* 4 (1978):93-96.

Freydorf, Roswith von. "James Welch, eine junge Stimme Alt-Amerikas," in *Mitteilungsblatt der Deutschen Gesellschaft für Amerikastudien.* Regensburg, 1975.

Horton, Andrew. "The Bitter Humor of *Winter in the Blood.*" *American Indian Quarterly* 4(1978):131-39.

Kunz, Don. "Lost in the Distance of Winter: James Welch's *Winter in the Blood.*" *Critique* 20(1978):93-99.

Larson, Charles R. *American Indian Fiction.* Albuquerque: University of New Mexico Press, 1978.

Lincoln, Kenneth. "Back-Tracking James Welch." *MELUS* 6(1979): 23-40.

Ruoff, A. LaVonne, ed. "A Discussion of *Winter in the Blood.*" *American Indian Quarterly* 4(1978):159-68.

————. "Alienation and the Female Principle in *Winter in the Blood.*" *American Indian Quarterly* 4(1978):107-122.

————. "History in *Winter in the Blood:* Backgrounds and Bibliography." *American Indian Quarterly* 4(1978):169-72.

Sands, Kathleen M. "Alienation and Broken Narrative in *Winter in the Blood.*" *American Indian Quarterly* 4(1978):97-105.

Smith, William F. "*Winter in the Blood:* The Indian Cowboy as Everyman." *Michigan Academician* 10(1978):299-306.

Velie, Alan R. "*Winter in the Blood* as Comic Novel." *American Indian Quarterly* 4(1978):141-47.

Leslie Silko

Larson, Charles R. *American Indian Fiction.* Albuquerque: University of New Mexico Press, 1978.

Ruoff, A. LaVonne. "Ritual and Renewal: Keres Traditions in the Short Fiction of Leslie Silko." *MELUS* 5(1978):2-17.

INDEX